Gianr

SANTORINI, THE ENCHANTED ISLAND
TREASURES AND WONDERS TO DISCOVER

*Itineraries, Flavors, and Unforgettable Views on the World's
Most Romantic Island*

"Suspended between the white of its houses and the infinite blue,
Santorini is a mosaic of light, shadow, and dreams to live."

Table of Contents

1. INTRODUCTION TO SANTORINI

1.1 Historical Notes on the Island

Originally called Thera, Santorini boasts a millennia-old history shaped by transformative events that left a lasting impact on its culture and landscape. Located in the heart of the Aegean Sea, the island has been inhabited since the Neolithic period but is best known for the catastrophic volcanic eruption of 1600 BCE. This event, one of the most powerful eruptions ever recorded, destroyed the thriving Minoan civilization in Akrotiri, burying it under volcanic ash that remarkably preserved its structures and artifacts. Some scholars link this eruption to the myth of Atlantis, further adding to the island's allure.

During the Classical period, Thera became an important commercial hub thanks to its strategic location. Over the centuries, it fell under the rule of various civilizations, including the Romans, Byzantines, Venetians, and Ottomans, each leaving their mark on its architectural and cultural heritage. During the Middle Ages, it was renamed Santorini by the Venetians in honor of Saint Irene, becoming a crucial maritime trading post.

Today, remnants of its past coexist with the breathtaking landscape of the caldera. The archaeological site of Akrotiri, the ancient city of Thera, and Venetian and Ottoman architectural influences are just some of the attractions that make Santorini a destination rich in history and culture.

1.2 Geography and Climate

Santorini, part of the Cyclades archipelago, is renowned for its extraordinary geological features and ideal Mediterranean climate, making it a highly sought-after destination. The island's unique landscape is the result of intense volcanic activity over millennia. At its heart lies the Caldera, a vast semicircular submerged crater formed during the 1600 BCE eruption.

Surrounding the caldera are striking tuff cliffs, rising up to 300 meters high, adorned with picturesque villages such as **Oia, Fira**, and Imerovigli, featuring the iconic whitewashed houses and blue-domed roofs.

Santorini's Mediterranean climate is characterized by hot, dry summers and mild, rainy winters. From May to September, temperatures range between 25°C and 35°C, accompanied by clear skies and a pleasant breeze, perfect for outdoor activities and beach relaxation. Winter, from November to March, is cooler, with temperatures between 10°C and 15°C, offering a quieter season for exploring the island without summer crowds.

Santorini offers a surprising variety of landscapes, from volcanic beaches with red, black, and white sands to fertile lands cultivated with vineyards and native cherry tomatoes. Its unique topography and favorable climate make it a natural wonder to explore in every season.

1.3 Why Visit Santorini

Santorini is a perfect blend of adventure, romance, and culture, offering an unforgettable experience for every traveler. It is one of the most charming and iconic destinations in the world, an island that combines breathtaking natural beauty, ancient history, and an unparalleled romantic atmosphere.

Located in the heart of the Aegean Sea, Santorini offers unique landscapes: its spectacular volcanic cliffs overlooking the caldera create an unforgettable view, especially at sunset when the sky is painted in warm colors and the view becomes pure magic. Villages like **Oia, Fira**, and **Imerovigli,** with their characteristic white houses and blue domes, represent the essence of the Cyclades and are perfect for romantic walks or dream-like photographs. Their welcoming atmosphere invites visitors to get lost in charming alleys and panoramic terraces offering unparalleled views.

Santorini is also an ideal destination for history and culture lovers, thanks to the archaeological site of **Akrotiri**, a Minoan city buried by a volcanic eruption and almost perfectly preserved over time. The island also hosts fascinating museums, such as the Museum of Prehistoric Thera, which

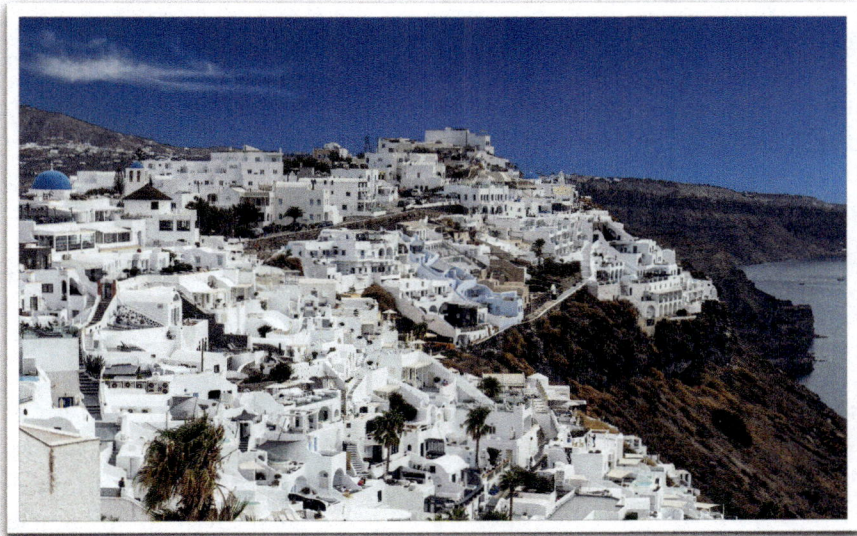

reveals the secrets of the Cycladic civilization and its inhabitants.

For those seeking relaxation, the island boasts unique beaches with red, black, and white sand, a result of its volcanic nature. Each beach offers a different atmosphere, from intimate, secluded bays to lively beach resorts with modern services. Strolling along the coast at sunset or swimming in the crystal-clear waters is pure poetry.

Wine and food enthusiasts can taste high-quality local wines, such as **Assyrtiko**, and traditional dishes prepared with local products like cherry tomatoes, fava, and white eggplant. A dinner with a view of the caldera, accompanied by a glass of local wine, is an experience that stays in your heart forever. There is no place in the world like Santorini, capable of enchanting anyone who steps foot on this Aegean wonder.

2. MAIN POINTS OF INTEREST

Santorini offers a wide range of attractions combining history, culture, nature, and spectacular views. Here are the must-visit places on the island.

2.1 Oia and Its Famous Sunset

Oia, perched at the northern tip of Santorini, is a jewel of the Cyclades archipelago, famous for its enchanting views and spectacular sunsets. This village is considered one of the most picturesque places in the world, attracting millions of visitors every year who wish to immerse themselves in its timeless magic.

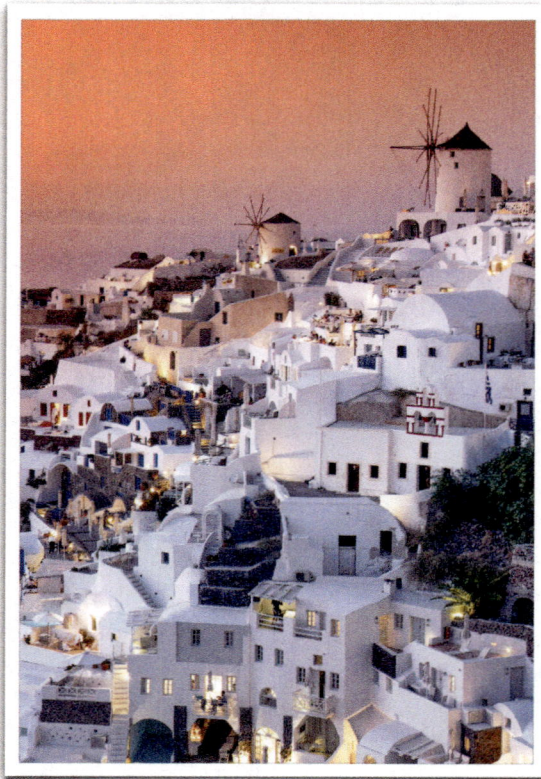

Characterized by Cycladic architecture, Oia is a maze of cobblestone streets, stairways climbing along the cliffs, and whitewashed houses, often carved directly into the volcanic rock. The traditional blue domes of the churches, the windmills, and the balconies overlooking the caldera add a fairy-tale touch to the landscape. Walking through its streets means immersing yourself in a romantic and relaxing atmosphere, surrounded by artisanal boutiques, art galleries, and small cafes offering panoramic views of the Aegean.

The sunset in Oia is an iconic event. Every evening, the village transforms into a natural stage for an unforgettable spectacle. The golden sunlight of sunset reflects off the white houses and the crystal-clear sea, creating a color palette ranging from fiery red to soft purple. The most popular viewpoints include the ruins of the Venetian castle in Oia, which offers an open view of the caldera, and the restaurants with panoramic terraces, where you can dine with a breathtaking backdrop.

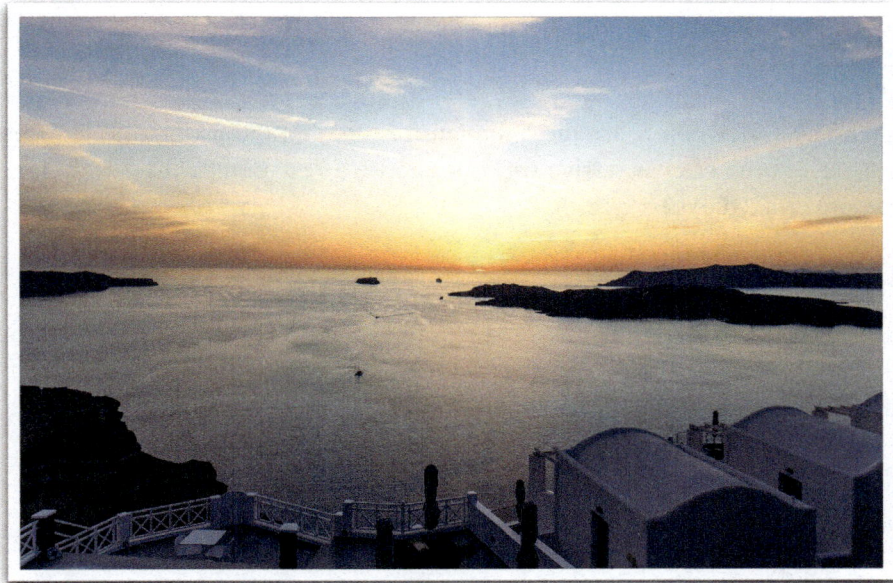

The sunset experience is not only visual but emotional. The moment when the sun dips below the horizon is often accompanied by a reverential silence, interrupted only by spontaneous applause from the crowd. It's a shared experience that brings together people from all over the world, united by the wonder of nature's beauty.

After sunset, the village lights up with soft lights and candles, creating an intimate and enchanting atmosphere.

Restaurants and tavernas come to life, offering local specialties such as the famous Assyrtiko wine or fresh fish dishes, perfect for concluding the evening.

Visiting Oia and experiencing its sunset is a memory that lasts forever. It is the symbol of Santorini's unique beauty, a place where nature, culture, and romance merge perfectly. A sunset in Oia is not just a moment of the day but an event that embodies the essence of the island.

Main Attractions:

O Oia Sunset

The best viewpoints are the Venetian fortress and the panoramic terraces. To avoid the crowds, arrive early or choose a restaurant with a view for a more relaxed experience.

O Blue Domed Churches

A symbol of Santorini, the blue-domed churches with white walls are located along the caldera. Be sure to visit the famous Panagia Platsani Church.

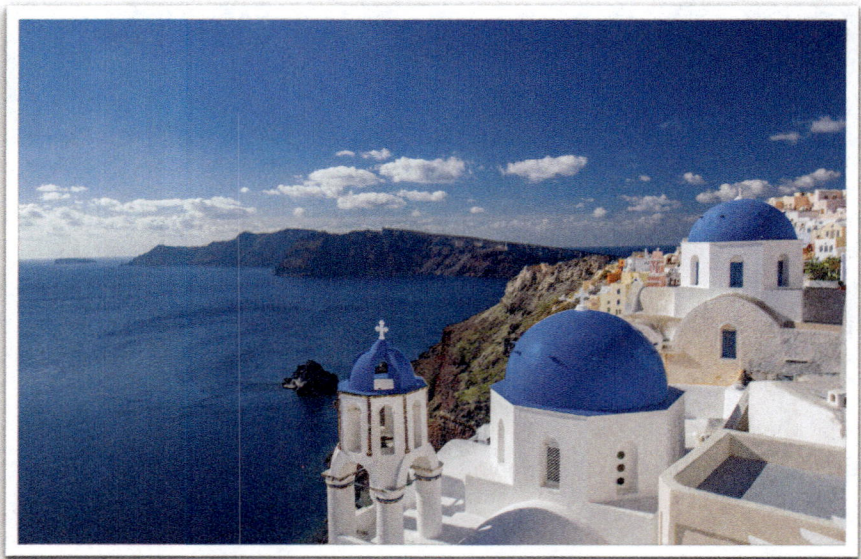

○ **Venetian Fortress**

This ancient ruined castle offers a panoramic view of the caldera and the village. It is also one of the most sought-after spots for sunset photos.

○ **Oia Windmills**

Located at the edge of the village, the windmills of Oia are another iconic sight in the area. Reach them for stunning photos, especially at sunset.

○ **Naval Museum of Oia**

Discover the maritime history of Santorini in this small but fascinating museum. Among the exhibits, you'll find ship models, navigational instruments, and historical paintings.

○ **Ammoudi Bay**

Located at the foot of Oia, this picturesque bay is reachable by descending a long staircase. Here you can swim in the crystal-clear waters and enjoy fresh fish at one of the seaside tavernas.

○ **Panoramic Walk**

Walking along the cobblestone streets of Oia is an experience in itself. Get lost among the alleys and boutiques, and explore art galleries, jewelry shops, and local craft stores.

Practical Tips:

1. **Arrive early or late**: During peak season, Oia can be extremely crowded. Visiting early in the morning or after sunset allows for a more peaceful exploration.

2. **Book in advance**: If you want to enjoy the sunset from a restaurant or panoramic terrace, make sure to book days in advance.

3. **Wear comfortable shoes**: The streets of Oia are cobbled and often steep, so choose shoes suitable for walking.

4. 11**Descend to Ammoudi Bay**: Bring a swimsuit if you want to swim, but remember the climb back is strenuous. You can opt for a taxi ride or rent a donkey to return (though this option is controversial for ethical reasons).

5. **Avoid the car**: The streets of Oia are narrow, and parking is difficult. Use public transportation or park outside the center and walk.

6. **Don't forget your camera**: Oia is one of the most photogenic villages in the world, so get ready to take lots of photos.

7. **Try the local cuisine**: Taste fresh fish at Ammoudi Bay or choose a tavern with a terrace to enjoy fava, capers, and the famous Vinsanto wine.

Oia is a dream experience, a place that combines natural beauty, unique architecture, and a romantic atmosphere. Take the time to savor every corner, letting yourself be enchanted by what makes it so special.

2.2 Fira and the Prehistoric Museum of Thera

Fira, the lively capital of Santorini, is the island's beating heart—a place where history, culture, and breathtaking panoramas come together. Perched on the caldera cliffs, Fira offers extraordinary views of the Aegean Sea and the volcanic islands of **Nea** and **Palea Kameni**. This village is a blend of tradition and modernity, with its whitewashed houses, blue-domed churches, and cobblestone streets bustling with shops, restaurants, bars, and boutiques, making it a must-visit destination on the island.

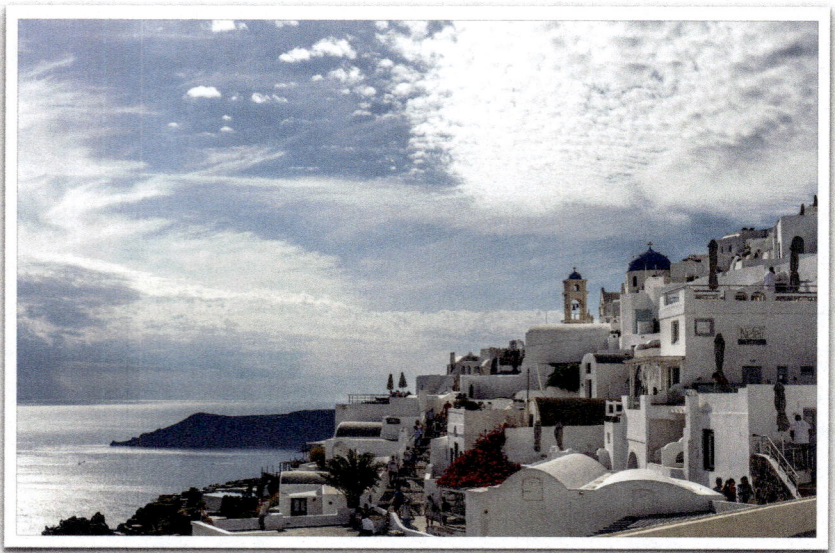

Strolling through Fira is a unique experience. You can explore picturesque alleys, visit local markets, and admire Cycladic architecture mingled with Venetian influences. In the evening, the city comes alive with enchanting lights and a vibrant nightlife. For romantic travelers, dining at one of the panoramic terrace restaurants offers the chance to enjoy an unforgettable view of the caldera.

One of Fira's highlights is the **Prehistoric Museum of Thera**, a cultural gem that narrates the ancient history of Santorini and is a must-see for history and culture enthusiasts.

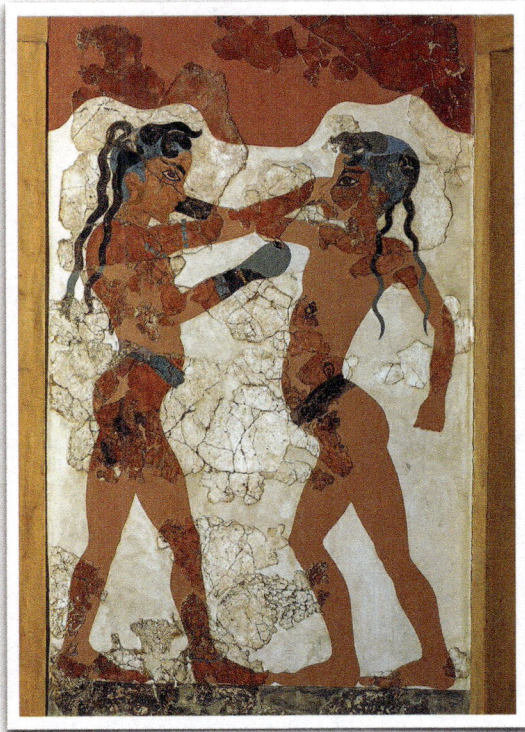

Located in the village center, the museum houses unique artifacts from the archaeological excavations at Akrotiri, a Minoan city buried by the volcanic eruption of 1600 BCE. Among the museum's most important treasures are the remarkably well-preserved frescoes, such as the famous *Fresco of the Young Boxers* and the *Fresco of the Seagulls.*

These paintings provide a glimpse into the daily life and religious beliefs of Santorini's ancient inhabitants. Visitors can also admire frescoes like the *Ladies of Akrotiri* and the *Blue Monkeys*, along with an imposing *pithos* (large terracotta jar) decorated with a bull.

Additionally, the museum exhibits ceramics, tools, weapons, and everyday objects that showcase the advanced Minoan civilization and its connections with other Aegean cultures. A notable feature is a three-dimensional model reconstructing the city of Akrotiri, illustrating how it appeared before the eruption. This helps visitors better understand the urban layout and advanced technology of the time.

Practical Information – Museum of Thera

- **Hours**: Open from April to October, 8:30 AM to 3:30 PM, closed on Tuesdays. Closed during winter (November to March) and on certain national holidays.
- **Tickets**: €6 for a single entry; €15 for a combined ticket valid for three days, including Akrotiri and the archaeological site of Thera.
- **How to get there**: The museum is located near Fira's central bus station, with free parking available nearby.

Tips

- Take advantage of the combined ticket to visit multiple archaeological sites.
- Plan your visit early in the morning to avoid crowds.
- If possible, join a guided tour for a deeper understanding of the exhibits.
- Wear comfortable shoes and consider stopping at one of Fira's cafes to relax after your visit.

Fira, with its museum and vibrancy, represents the perfect balance between historical heritage and modernity. It's a place that satisfies both culture lovers and those seeking relaxation and fun, making it an essential stop for anyone visiting Santorini. The combination of breathtaking panoramas, fascinating history, and dynamic atmosphere makes Fira one of the island's most memorable destinations.

Main Attractions in Fira

- **The View of the Caldera**
  The cliffside view from Fira is one of Santorini's most iconic. From the main promenade, you can admire the submerged volcanic crater and the Aegean Sea, especially during sunset.

- **The Archaeological Museum of Thera**
  This museum houses artifacts from the Minoan civilization excavated from Akrotiri, as well as sculptures and ceramics that narrate the island's ancient history. A must-visit for history enthusiasts.

- **The Prehistoric Museum of Thera**
  A must-see exhibit of Minoan frescoes, including the famous *Blue Monkeys Fresco* and other unique artifacts dating back to the prehistoric period.

- **The Metropolitan Orthodox Cathedral**
  This imposing church, with its elegant arches and white dome, is a symbol of Fira. Inside, visitors will find fascinating frescoes and decorations.

- **The Santorini Cable Car**
  For a fun and scenic experience, take the cable car connecting Fira to the old port. It's a charming alternative to the long staircase.

- **The Nightlife**
  Fira is the center of Santorini's nightlife, with bars and clubs like the famous "Tropical Bar" and "Koo Club" where you can party late into the night.

- **Shopping in Local Boutiques**

  Along Fira's alleys, you'll find jewelry, clothing, and local crafts. Don't miss shops selling Santorini's famous wine or products made with tomatoes and capers.

Visiting Tips

1. **Plan your visit early in the morning or at sunset**: Fira can be very crowded during peak hours. For a stress-free experience, choose quieter times.

2. **Wear comfortable shoes**: Fira's streets are cobblestone and steep in some areas.

3. **Use public transport**: Fira's central bus station is well-connected to other villages on Santorini. It's an economical and practical option.

4. **Stay sun-safe**: Always carry hats, sunglasses, and sunscreen, especially during summer visits.

5. **Try panoramic restaurants**: For a unique dining experience, choose a tavern with a view of the caldera, like "Argo Restaurant" or "Naoussa".Fira is the ideal starting point for exploring the island and immersing yourself in its unique charm. Plan carefully to fully enjoy its vibrancy and romance!

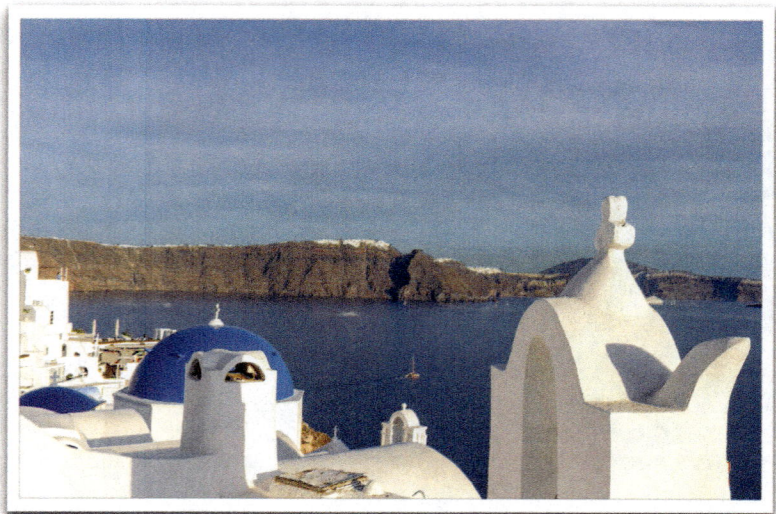

2.3 Imerovigli and Panoramic Views

Imerovigli, known as the "balcony of the Aegean," is a picturesque village perched atop Santorini's caldera, about 3 kilometers from Fira. Renowned for its spectacular views, it's one of the island's highest points, offering breathtaking panoramas of the Aegean Sea, the caldera, and the volcano.

This tranquil village is characterized by traditional white houses, narrow cobblestone alleys, and blue-domed churches. Less crowded than Fira and Oia, Imerovigli is the perfect spot for those seeking peace and an authentic experience away from the bustling tourist areas.

Panoramic Views

Imerovigli's privileged position offers unparalleled views throughout the day. At sunset, the sky is painted with shades of pink and orange, creating a natural spectacle that attracts photographers and romantics from around the world. The view stretches toward the volcanic islands of Nea and Palea Kameni, surrounded by the crystal-clear waters of the Aegean, with the imposing caldera as the backdrop.One of the village's most iconic landmarks is **Skaros Rock**, a rocky formation that once housed a Venetian castle. Accessible via a panoramic trail, Skaros offers spectacular views of the caldera and the surrounding villages. The hike to the rock is a must-do for nature and photography enthusiasts.

Curiosities and Activities

O **Weddings and Honeymoons**: Imerovigli is a favorite destination for weddings and romantic getaways, thanks to its intimate atmosphere and extraordinary terrace views.

O **Traditional Churches**: Don't miss the Church of Ai-Stratis, located near Skaros, and other charming chapels scattered throughout the village.

O **Panoramic Dining**: Many restaurants and boutique hotels offer terraces with views, perfect for a sunset dinner.

Visiting Tips

O Wear comfortable shoes for exploring the panoramic trails and Skaros Rock.

O Visit at sunset to witness the caldera's spectacular colors.

O Book in advance if you wish to dine at one of the restaurants with a view.

With its serene beauty and dreamy vistas, Imerovigli captivates visitors. Perfect for relaxation and enjoying the magic of Santorini, it's a must-visit destination for those seeking unforgettable experiences on the island.

2.4 Akrotiri and the Archaeological Site

The archaeological site of Akrotiri, located in southern Santorini, is one of the island's most precious treasures and among the most significant archaeological discoveries in the Aegean. Often compared to Pompeii, Akrotiri is a prehistoric Minoan city buried under layers of volcanic ash following the devastating eruption of 1600 BCE. This natural preservation has remarkably protected buildings, frescoes, and many artifacts, offering a detailed glimpse into the daily life of an ancient civilization.

Akrotiri dates back to the Neolithic period but reached its peak during the Minoan era, becoming a major commercial and cultural center.

Thanks to excavations begun in 1967 by archaeologist Spyridon Marinatos, visitors can admire the remains of a highly organized city with multi-story buildings, paved streets, advanced drainage systems, and highly refined artistic decorations.

One of the most stunning features of the site is its frescoes. Although many are displayed in the Prehistoric Museum of Thera, some fragments can be seen directly at Akrotiri. These paintings depict scenes of daily life, nature, animals, and maritime activities, highlighting Akrotiri's connection to the sea.

The frescoes such as *"The Swallows"* and *"Spring"* reveal the artistic skill and aesthetic taste of the Minoan civilization

La Primavera

The archaeological site is covered by a modern structure that protects the remains and allows visitors to explore the ancient city through elevated walkways. This setup enables a close view of houses, storage rooms, workshops, and streets, offering an immersive journey into the past.Akrotiri is also famous for its connection to the mystery of Atlantis. Some scholars believe the city may have inspired the myth of Atlantis, given its sudden decline and advanced development.

Visiting Akrotiri is like traveling back in time—a unique opportunity to understand the complexity and innovation of the Minoan civilization. The site fascinates not only archaeology enthusiasts but also anyone eager to discover an extraordinary chapter in Mediterranean history. It's a must-see for anyone visiting Santorini, combining beauty, history, and mystery.

Opening Hours and Visitor Tips for Akrotiri Archaeological Site

Opening Hours:

- **High season (April 1 - October 31):** Open daily from 8:00 AM to 8:00 PM.
- **Low season (November 6 - March 31):** Open Tuesday to Sunday, from 8:00 AM to 3:00 PM. Closed on Mondays during this period.
- **Free Entry:** On specific days, such as International Monuments Day (April 18), International Museum Day (May 18), and certain national holidays.

Tickets:

- €12 for adults, €6 for students and EU citizens over 65.
  A €15 combined ticket valid for three days includes the Prehistoric Museum of Thera in Fira and the Ancient Thera site.

Visitor Tips:

1. **Arrive early:** During high season, visiting in the morning helps avoid crowds and the afternoon heat.
2. **Book a guide:** The site is rich in historical and archaeological details best understood with an expert guide. Italian-speaking guides can be booked in advance at the ticket office.
3. **Combine with the Prehistoric Museum of Thera:** Located in Fira, this museum displays many frescoes and artifacts from Akrotiri, providing broader context for the archaeological site.

4. **Stay hydrated and wear comfortable shoes:** While the site is covered and well-ventilated, walking along the pathways can be time-consuming.

5. **Consider a combined tour**: Some tours also include nearby attractions, such as beaches and Santorini's famous vineyards.

Akrotiri is a one-of-a-kind experience that offers a glimpse into the life of an advanced civilization preserved for millennia under volcanic ash. Combine the visit with other cultural and natural attractions on the island for a complete experience.

2.5 Pyrgos, the Traditional Village

Situated on a hill in the heart of Santorini, Pyrgos is one of the island's most authentic and charming villages. Far from the hustle and bustle of Fira and Oia, Pyrgos retains a calm and genuine atmosphere that tells the story and traditions of the island.

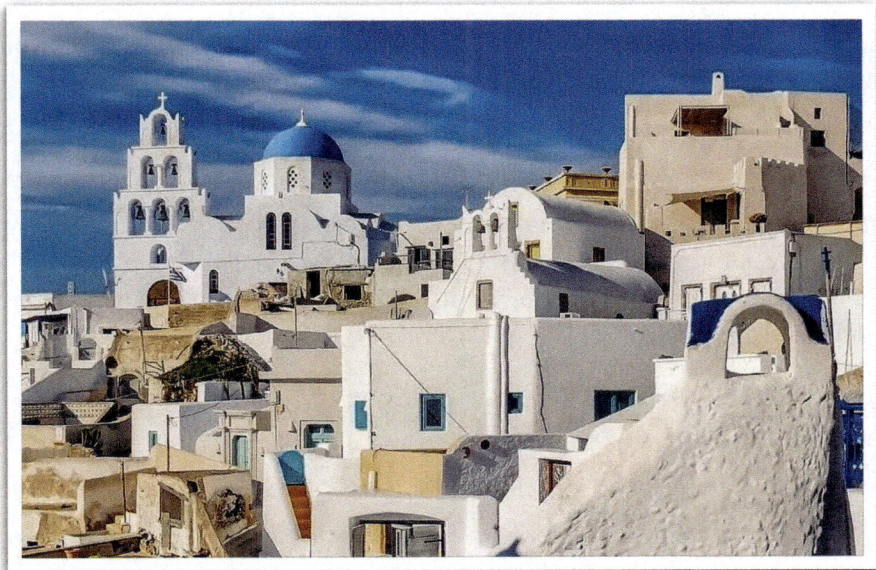

Known for its labyrinthine alleys, white houses, and breathtaking panoramic views, this village is a must-visit for those wanting to discover the most authentic soul of Santorini.

A Journey into History

Pyrgos was the ancient capital of Santorini and stands out for its medieval structure. dominated by a Venetian castle, the Kastro. This historical complex, dating back to the 15th century, offers a fascinating journey into the past, with fortified walls, ancient churches, and picturesque glimpses. As you ascend towards the castle, you pass narrow and winding alleys, perfect for getting lost and discovering hidden corners. From the top, the panoramic view of the island is spectacular, especially at sunset when the sky turns shades of pink and orange.

Main Attractions

In addition to the Kastro, Pyrgos boasts an abundance of historical churches, such as the Theotokaki Church, one of the oldest on the island. For art and history lovers, the Prophet Elias Museum, located at the eponymous monastery a short distance from the village, is an interesting visit. Here, you can admire religious artifacts, ancient texts, and traditional tools.

Atmosphere and Cuisine

Walking through Pyrgos, you breathe in an authentic and relaxed atmosphere. The local tavernas serve typical Greek dishes, such as moussaka, Santorini fava, and stuffed tomatoes, accompanied by the island's famous wine. Franco's Café, with its panoramic terrace, is perfect for sipping a cocktail at sunset.

<u>Tips for Visiting</u>

1. Wear comfortable shoes: the alleys are uphill and often cobbled.

2. Visit at sunset: the view from the top of the village is spectacular.

3. Take your time: Pyrgos is not a place to rush; take a relaxing stroll to soak in the atmosphere.

4. Explore the surroundings: The Prophet Elias Monastery, just a few minutes' drive away, offers incredible views and is a peaceful spot.

Pyrgos is ideal for those seeking an authentic experience away from the crowds, where history, culture, and tradition blend with the natural beauty of Santorini. A place that invites you to slow down and enjoy every moment.

3. THE VOLCANIC BEACHES OF SANTORINI

Santorini's beaches are famous for their unique charm, characterized by sand and pebbles in extraordinary shades that derive from the volcanic origin of the island. These beaches differ from the classic sandy stretches of the Aegean Sea with their intense colors, ranging from black to red and white, offering breathtaking landscapes and an almost lunar atmosphere. Each beach has its own personality and deserves to be explored.

Santorini's beaches are not only places for relaxation but also authentic natural wonders that tell the geological and cultural history of the island. Here is an overview of the best beaches, with details on how to reach them, the services offered, and the costs.

With its extraordinary variety of beaches, Santorini offers unforgettable experiences for all tastes.

Main Beaches

3.1 Red Beach

It is one of the most iconic beaches on the island thanks to its spectacular red volcanic rocks that contrast with the deep blue of the sea. Located near the village of Akrotiri, it is easily accessible by car or bus from Fira.

How to Reach It

Buses stop near the Akrotiri archaeological site, from which you walk for about 10-15 minutes along a moderately steep path to reach the beach, so it's advisable to wear suitable shoes.

Alternatively, you can reach it by sea with taxi-boats available every half hour (about €5 one way).

Services and Facilities

Red Beach is a semi-organized beach: it offers umbrellas and sunbeds at an average cost of €10-20, managed by local operators, but they are not always guaranteed due to limited space.

There are no fully equipped structures on the beach, but you'll find a small kiosk where you can buy drinks and snacks.

It is advisable to bring water, snacks, and an umbrella, as the food services are scarce or limited to street vendors.

The beach is small and tends to be very crowded, especially during the high season, so arriving early is essential to find a spot.

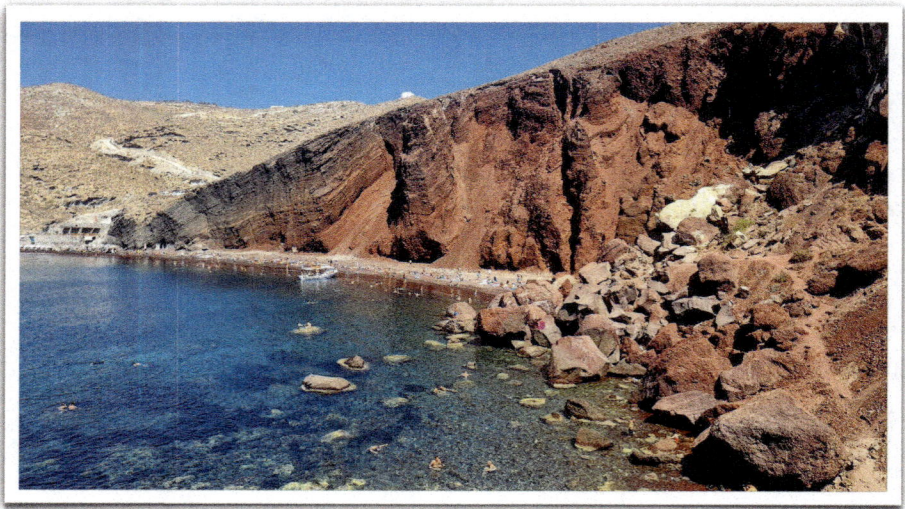

Sea water quality

The sea is clear, with a seabed rich in red and black pebbles, ideal for snorkeling. However, the beach is exposed to higher waves during the low season, and attention is needed for currents, which can be moderate on windy days.

Activities and Entertainment

Red Beach is ideal for swimming and snorkeling, but there are no structured activities like water sports. It can be combined with a visit to the nearby

Akrotiri archaeological site or a boat trip to the nearby White Beach. The red cliffs surrounding the area offer a unique backdrop for memorable photographs.

Tips
- **Safety:** The area is prone to landslides, so it's important to pay attention to danger signs and weather conditions. Some prefer to admire the beach from above without descending to the shore.
- **Timing:** Visit early in the morning or during the low season to avoid crowds.
- **Alternative Transportation:** Consider a catamaran tour that includes a stop for swimming at Red Beach, avoiding the crowded and potentially dangerous paths.
- **Bring suitable** shoes for the path and don't forget sunscreen and water.

The red cliffs surrounding the area offer a unique backdrop for memorable photos, but it's less suitable for spending an entire day of relaxation due to the lack of extensive infrastructure and limited space.

Note: The beach is often overcrowded due to its small size. As a result, it is not always clean. It's advisable, as mentioned earlier, to arrive early and move to other nearby beaches if it becomes too crowded.

The closest beach to Red Beach in Santorini is **Kampia Beach** It is just a few minutes' walk from Red Beach and can also be reached by sea with a taxi boat. Kampia is less crowded and quieter, ideal for those seeking a more secluded experience. It is famous for its dark sand and crystal-clear waters, making it a perfect spot for swimming and snorkeling.

Kampia lacks extensive services or tourist facilities. There are no umbrellas or sunbeds available, so it's advisable to bring everything you need, such as water, food, and sunscreen.

If you prefer a more organized beach with better amenities, Perissa (described below) is one of the nearby beaches, though not immediately adjacent to Red Beach (approximately a 10-minute drive or taxi ride).

3.2 Black Beach (Perissa and Perivolos)

The beaches of **Perissa** and **Perivolos** form part of the so-called **"Black Beach,"** located on the southeastern coast of Santorini. Both feature the characteristic black volcanic sand and a lively atmosphere.

These long, spacious beaches with black volcanic sand are perfect for families and groups of friends and are among the most iconic on the island.

How to Get There

Located approximately 13 km from Fira, Black Beach is accessible via a road that branches off towards the Akrotiri lighthouse. You can get there by public bus, car, taxi, or scooter.

- **By Bus**: Buses operate frequently throughout the day, with a journey time of about 20-25 minutes and a ticket price of €2.20 per trip. Regular service is available daily from 7:00 AM to midnight, making it convenient for evening visits or dining at local restaurants.

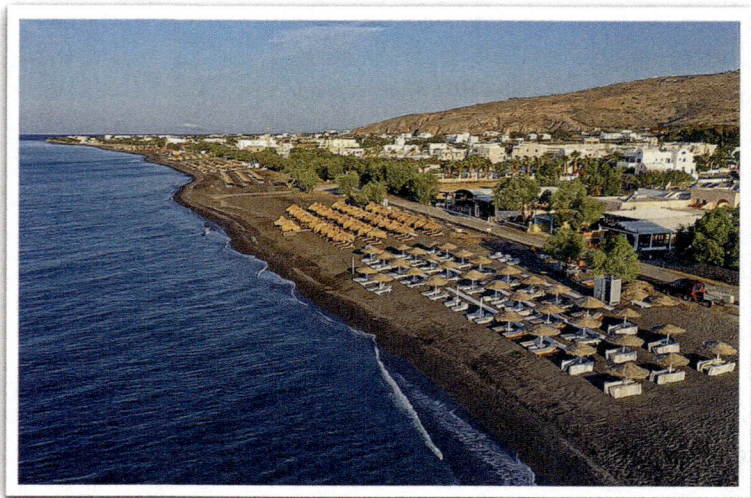

- **By Car**: A small free parking lot is available nearby, though it fills up quickly during peak season.
- **On Foot**: Those relying on public transport can take a bus to Pyrgos and then walk a short distance.

Facilities and Amenities

This is one of the best-equipped beaches in Santorini, offering sunbeds, umbrellas, and food services at numerous beach establishments. Beach bars and restaurants serve local dishes, adding to the experience.

- **Perissa**: With its many beach bars and restaurants, Perissa offers a semi-organized setting. Sunbeds and umbrellas are generally available for rent at around €15-20 for two people but are often complimentary with food or drink purchases.
- **Perivolos**: A natural extension of Perissa, Perivolos is quieter and ideal for those seeking a more relaxed atmosphere. It is easily reachable via a coastal walk or by car, with well-marked roads. Perivolos also boasts a more exclusive vibe, featuring trendy spots and live music.

Sea water Quality

The waters are crystal clear, deep, and perfect for swimming. Be cautious, as the black sand can become very hot; beach shoes are recommended.

Activities and Entertainment

- **Water Sports**: Options include jet skiing, parasailing, and paddleboarding.
- **Beach Parties**: Especially at Perivolos during the summer months.
- **Excursions**: Boats departing from Perissa harbor head to Red Beach and other destinations.
- **Seaside Walks**: Ideal for a romantic evening stroll, with shops, bars, and venues enlivening the area.

> **Tips**
> 1. **Swim Safely**: Be cautious of strong currents in some areas and follow local authorities' guidance.
> 2. **Wear Beach Shoes**: The hot sand and rocky areas make sturdy footwear essential.
> 3. **Explore**: Take a walk along the Perissa promenade for souvenirs, bars, and gelato.
> 4. **Try Local Cuisine**: Enjoy traditional Greek dishes at beachside restaurants. Must-try dishes include moussaka, gyros, and Greek salad.

3.3 White Beach

Located on Santorini's southern coast near Red Beach, White Beach is accessible only by boat or via a challenging footpath.

The beach is known for its white cliffs and light pebbles, contrasting beautifully with the turquoise waters. It offers a tranquil experience, less crowded than other Santorini beaches, perfect for relaxation or snorkeling among underwater caves and picturesque rocks.

How to Get There

- **By Boat**: Regular boat services operate from Akrotiri port and nearby beaches like Perissa and Kamari. The boat ride takes approximately 15 minutes and costs €10-15 round trip.

- **On Foot**: A 20-30 minute hike from Red Beach leads to White Beach, though the path is somewhat challenging.

Facilities and Amenities

A small tavern serves traditional Greek dishes, making it a great spot for lunch. Sunbeds and umbrellas can be rented for €15-20 per day. Early arrival is recommended, as the beach is small and fills up quickly during high season.

Sea water quality

The waters are exceptionally clear, with turquoise hues contrasting against the surrounding white cliffs. The seabed is ideal for diving and snorkeling.

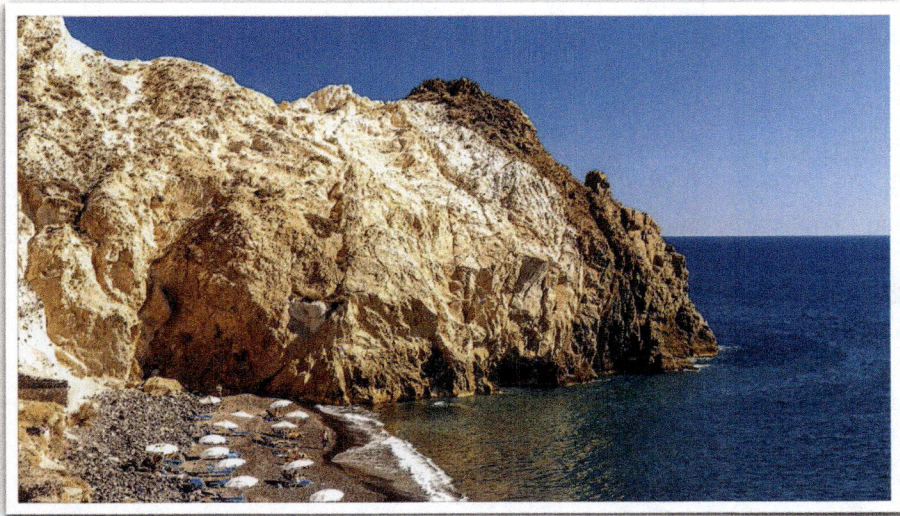

Activities and Entertainment

White Beach is perfect for those seeking peace and relaxation, away from crowds.

Photography: Capture the wind-sculpted rock formations, white cliffs, and marine caves.

Tips
- **Safety**: Entering the water can be tricky due to pebbles, so exercise caution.
- **Visit Early**: Enjoy the tranquility of the morning hours.
- **Respect Nature**: Bring a bag for waste and keep the beach pristine.
- **Including White Beach** in a boat tour that also visits Red Beach and Kampia is an excellent way to explore Santorini's iconic beaches with out worrying about logistics.

3.4 Kamari

Situated near the airport on the southeastern coast, Kamari is one of the island's most popular destinations, known for its beauty and well-equipped facilities. Kamari features black sand and dark pebbles typical of the area, making beach footwear essential. The 2-km-long beach lies at the base of Mesa Vouno, offering a unique and picturesque backdrop.

How to Get There
Easily accessible from Fira (10 km) by bus, taxi, or rental car. It is also a short distance from the airport.

Sea water quality
The sea at Kamari is crystal clear and deep just a few steps from the shore, making it ideal for swimming and diving. The beach has been awarded the Blue Flag, ensuring high standards of cleanliness and safety.

Facilities and Amenities

Kamari is a fully equipped beach with umbrellas and sunbeds available for €15-25 per day. Restaurants, bars, and taverns along the shoreline offer both local and international cuisine. The pedestrian-only promenade is perfect for relaxing walks and shopping at small stores.

Activities and Entertainment

- **Water Sports**: Snorkeling, paddleboarding, and diving.
- **Hiking**: Visit the Ancient Thira archaeological site on Mesa Vouno.

Tips

- **Best Time to Visit**: June and September are quieter months, avoiding the peak summer crowds.
- **Avoid the North End**: Proximity to the airport may result in noise from air traffic.
- **Book Ahead**: Reserve sunbeds or accommodations early, as Kamari is very popular.

3.5 Vlychada

Located in southern Santorini, about 14 km from Fira, Vlychada is known as **"Moon Beach"** due to its unique white cliffs sculpted by wind and sea, giving it a lunar appearance.

The 800-meter-long beach features dark volcanic sand and pebbles, with crystal-clear waters that quickly become deep, making it ideal for experienced swimmers and snorkeling enthusiasts.

How to Get There

It can be accessed by car, taxi, or bus. If driving, follow the signs to Vlychada from the main road to Akrotiri. The beach is also served by buses departing from Fira, but it's recommended to inform the driver of your destination, as stops may vary.

Facilities and Amenities

Vlychada offers a peaceful and uncrowded atmosphere, with a limited selection of umbrellas and sunbeds mainly available on the eastern side (€10-20 per set on average), while free areas are also present. A free parking area is nearby. The beach features a tavern and a snack bar serving Greek dishes and drinks, providing the chance to enjoy spectacular sunsets.

Sea water quality

The water is clean and perfect for relaxation or water activities, though its sudden depths and possible currents may not be suitable for families with small children. For a more secluded experience, continue along the beach to find more isolated areas, some frequented by naturists.

Activities and Entertainment
- Relaxation and nature immersion in a tranquil setting.
- Visit the Tomato Museum, located nearby, for a unique cultural experience.
- Hiking along the cliffs to admire the landscape.

Tips

- Bring food and water if you plan to stay in less-equipped areas.

- The beach is perfect for stunning sunsets and moments of relaxation away from the crowd.

- Nearby, you can visit the Tomato Museum of Vlychada, a fascinating cultural attraction showcasing the island's tomato production history. If you love exploring, take a stroll along the seafront or visit the nearby marina.

Vlychada is an ideal destination for those seeking natural beauty and tranquility, far from Santorini's busier areas.

Ammoudi Bay

This is not a traditional beach but a rocky bay perfect for swimming in crystal-clear waters and enjoying romantic seafood dining right by the water. Located at the foot of Oia, it's one of Santorini's most picturesque spots. This small circular port is famous for its breathtaking views. There are no sunbeds or umbrellas, making it ideal for those seeking an authentic and unique experience.

How to Get There
- **From Oia on foot:** Walk down a rocky path of approximately 214 steps. This is a great option for those who enjoy physical activity and want to take in spectacular views along the descent.
- **By mule:** If you prefer to avoid walking, you can take a mule ride to reach the bay.

- **From Fira:** Take a bus to Oia and continue on foot along the trail to Ammoudi Bay.
- **From Akrotiri:** Take a bus to Oia, then follow the footpath to Ammoudi Bay.

Sea water quality

The waters are clear and deep, ideal for a refreshing swim. There are no facilities like sunbeds or umbrellas, but you can relax on the rocks.

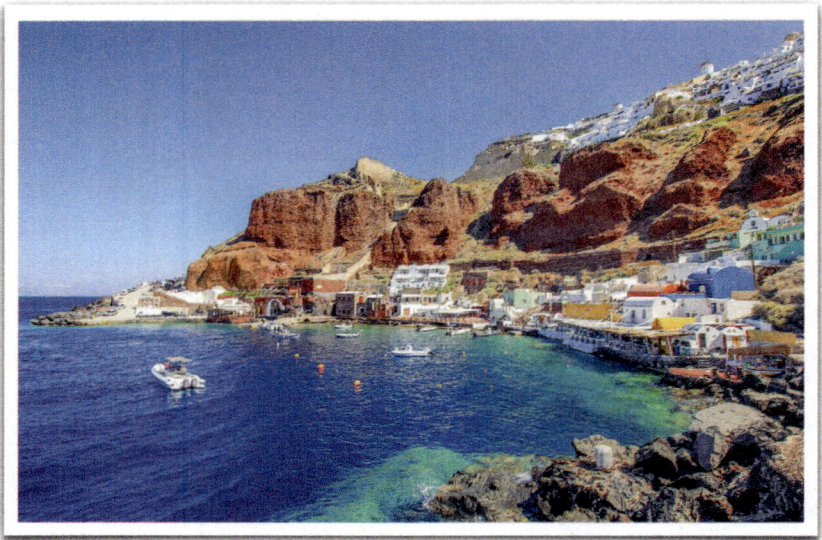

Activities and Entertainment

- **Swimming and snorkeling:** Perfect for exploring the marine life in crystal-clear waters.
- **Fishing:** Many visit Ammoudi Bay for fishing and outdoor dining.
- **Excursions:** The bay is an ideal starting point for boat trips to other beaches and caves.

Facilities and Amenities

- **Traditional Taverns:** Ammoudi Bay has around 7-10 seaside restaurants specializing in fresh fish and Greek dishes, including Ammoudi Fish Tavern, Taverna Katina, and Sunset Ammoudi by Paraskevas.
- **Cliff jumping and swimming:** Beyond the restaurants, you'll find ideal spots for swimming and cliff diving. The small island of St. Nicholas, visible from the bay, is a popular spot for cliff diving. Water shoes are recommended for safety.
- **Unique sunsets:** Ammoudi is one of the best places to watch the sunset, especially from a tavern terrace.

Practical Tips

- **Reservations:** For sunset dining, book in advance as restaurants fill up quickly.
- **Comfortable shoes:** Wear them for walking the stairs and rocky trails.
- **Budget:** Restaurants in Ammoudi Bay tend to be pricey, with main courses starting at €30-40.

Ammoudi Bay is perfect for those seeking a mix of Greek tradition, spectacular scenery, and authentic flavors.

3.7 Monolithos Beach

Monolithos Beach, located on the eastern coast of Santorini, is approximately 9 km from Fira and close to the village of Kamari. This beach is perfect for families due to its shallow waters and the presence of playgrounds for children. The black and grey volcanic sand stretches over a long surface, offering both organized areas and quieter, more secluded spots.

How to Get There

Monolithos is easily accessible by car, taxi, or bus from Fira's central station. Direct buses run three times a day, but it's advisable to inform the driver of your destination. The beach is also close to the national airport, making it convenient for those arriving or departing from the island.

Sea water quality

The waters at Monolithos are clear and ideal for swimming, thanks to the shallow seabed. The beach's tranquility and spaciousness make it an excellent choice for those seeking peace away from the island's busier spots.

Facilities and Amenities

The beach is partially equipped with umbrellas and sunbeds, usually available for rent starting at 10-15 euros per day. It is popular among families due to the shallow waters and a playground. There is a lifeguard station, football and volleyball fields, and several kiosks and taverns offering Greek dishes. For those seeking relaxation, the less organized area provides natural shade from the trees. It's also a great option for water sports such as windsurfing and kitesurfing.

Several taverns and cafes along the beach serve local food and cocktails. Recommended options include Captain Loizos Fish Restaurant and Taverna Skaramagkas.

3.8 Cape Columbo Beach

Cape Columbo is located in the northeastern part of Santorini, about 4 km from Oia. It is one of the island's most wild, untouched, and tranquil beaches, characterized by dark sand mixed with pebbles and impressive cliffs that shield it from the wind. This secluded beach offers a more rugged experience for those seeking solitude.

How to Get There

It is best reached by car or scooter, following signs to Cape Columbo from Oia. Parking is available nearby, but you'll need to walk a short path to access the beach.

Facilities and Amenities

This beach is not equipped with facilities, so you won't find umbrellas, sunbeds, or food services. It's recommended to bring everything you need, including water and snacks. The lack of structures makes Cape Columbo ideal for an authentic, immersive experience in nature.

Sea water quality

The waters are crystal-clear and often calm, but it's essential to be cautious of occasional currents. The beach is sparsely populated, making it perfect for those seeking isolation and a wild atmosphere.

Activities and Entertainment

- **Paddleboarding and Kayaking:** Perfect for enjoying the sea in a relaxed yet adventurous way.
- **Windsurfing:** Popular among enthusiasts thanks to constant winds.
- **Hiking:** The surrounding area offers interesting trails for walks

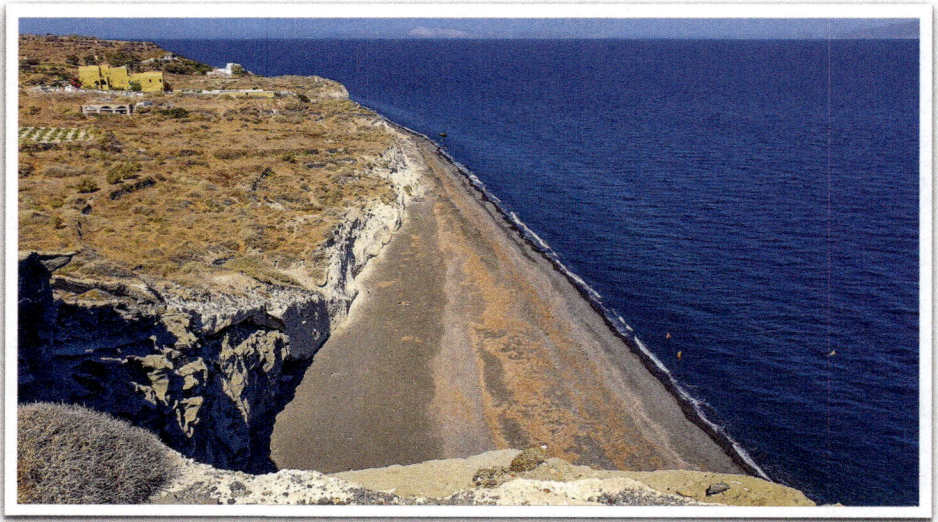

Tips for Monolithos and Cape Columbo Beach

1. **Monolithos Beach** is near the Monolithos Castle, a historic attraction with breathtaking panoramic views.

2. **At Monolithos**, visit the nearby village for an authentic local experience.

3. At Cape Columbo, wear comfortable shoes for the path and prepare for a rustic and serene atmosphe

4. **For couples:** the secluded nature of Cape Columbo makes it a romantic choice for couples looking for a private moment. Bring a blanket and organize a small picnic on the beach for a special experience.

5. **Beware of the Currents**: waters at Cape Columbo can be deep, and currents may be strong, so exercise caution if you decide to swim. Note that there are no lifeguards on-site

6. **Camera:** Ensure your camera or smartphone is ready to capture stunning landscapes and sunsets.

Beaches: Fun Facts and General Tips

The volcanic beaches of Santorini are not only relaxing spots but also natural wonders that reflect the island's geological and cultural history.

- **Therapeutic Properties:** Volcanic sand is rich in minerals beneficial for the skin. Walking barefoot or lying on the sand can be a rejuvenating experience.

- **Sand Temperature:** During summer, the black sand quickly absorbs the sun's heat, making it very hot. It's advisable to bring suitable footwear for comfortable walking.

- **Water Sports:** Many beaches, such as Kamari and Perivolos, offer activities like windsurfing, jet skiing, and scuba diving

General Tips:

▷ Bring water, sunscreen, and an umbrella if visiting less-equipped beaches like Red Beach or White Beach.

▷ To explore multiple beaches in one day, consider a boat tour, which often includes snorkeling stops and unique views of volcanic cliffs.

▷ **Footwear:** Black sand beaches become very hot under the sun; bring appropriate shoes.

▷ **Transportation:** Main beaches are connected by buses, but renting a car offers more flexibility.

▷ **Equipment:** Sunbeds and umbrellas typically cost 10-20 €, though many beach bars offer them for free with a purchase.

▷ **Timing:** Arrive early, especially at popular beaches, to avoid crowds and secure parking.

▷ **Restaurants:** Every beach features taverns and bars for meals or cocktails; try local specialties like fava beans and fresh fish.

4. EXCURSIONS AND ACTIVITIES

Santorini is an island that blends spectacular landscapes, ancient culture, and a unique atmosphere, making it an ideal destination for unforgettable experiences. The excursions and activities offered reflect the island's rich volcanic history, charming traditions, and natural beauty of the Aegean Sea. From sunset cruises in the caldera to tastings of fine wines, every activity is an opportunity to discover a different side of this Cycladic gem.

Exploring Santorini means diving into a variety of experiences, ranging from adventure and nature discovery to relaxation and culinary delights. Archaeological tours allow you to walk through the island's ancient history, while hiking along its panoramic trails offers breathtaking views. Additionally, volcanic seabeds and unique beaches provide numerous opportunities for water sports and moments of pure relaxation.

4.1. Boat Tours Around the Caldera

One of the most iconic experiences is exploring the volcanic caldera by boat. Cruises often include:

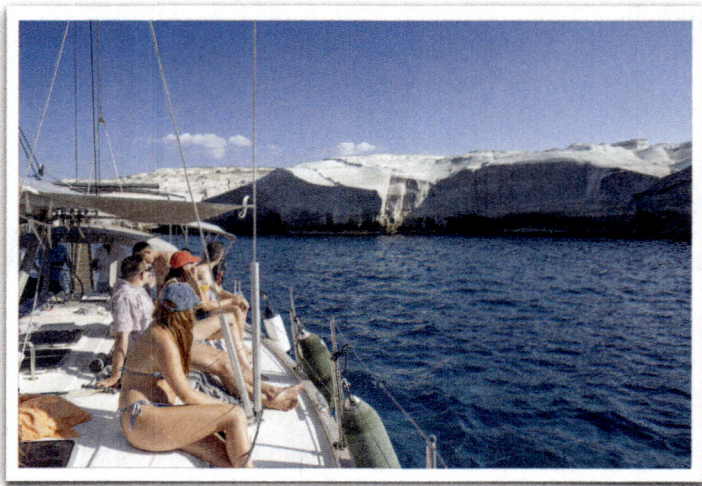

- **Visits to the volcanoes** of Nea Kameni and Palea Kameni, where you can hike to the active crater.
- **Stops at the hot springs** of Palea Kameni, where sulfur-rich waters offer a rejuvenating bath.
- **Sunset Cruises:** Evening tours with spectacular views of the sun setting behind the caldera.

4.2. Cultural Experiences and Archaeological Visits

- **Akrotiri:** A well-preserved Minoan city, often compared to Pompeii, offering an immersion into the island's history.
- **Ancient Thera:** Located on a hill above Kamari, it features breathtaking views and historical ruins from the Hellenistic, Roman, and Byzantine eras.
- **Museums and Art Galleries:** The Museum of Prehistoric Thera and the Archaeological Museum of Fira are must-sees.
- **Traditional Events:** Participate in local festivals to experience traditional music, dance, and cuisine.

4.3. Nature Excursions

- **Hiking from Fira to Oia:** A scenic 10 km trail that passes through volcanic landscapes and picturesque villages, offering incredible caldera views.
- **Cape Columbo and Red Beach:** Ideal for hikes in less crowded natural spots.

4.4. Wine and Gastronomy Tours

- **Winery Tours:** Santorini is famous for Assyrtiko wine, made from grapes grown in volcanic soil. Many wineries offer tastings and guided tours.
- **Greek Cooking Classes:** Santorini's cuisine reflects its volcanic roots and Cycladic traditions. Learn to prepare traditional dishes like moussaka, fava, and dolmades.

4.5. Water Sports and Outdoor Activities

▷ **Snorkeling and Diving:** Near Perissa, Kamari, or the caldera, explore volcanic seabeds.

▷ **Kitesurfing and Windsurfing:** At Monolithos and Perivolos, where winds are ideal.

▷ **Kayaking or Paddleboarding:** Discover coastal caves and hidden shores

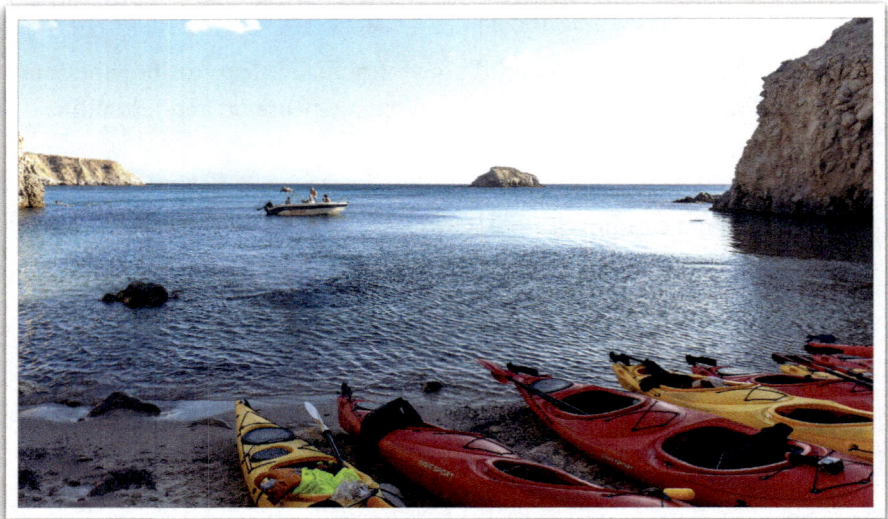

Practical Tips

▷ **Bookings:** For popular cruises and activities, book in advance, especially during high season.

▷ **Clothing:** Bring comfortable shoes for hiking and archaeological tours, and sunscreen for outdoor activities.

▷ **Transport:** Many activities include transportation to/from your accommodation, but renting a car or scooter is useful for independent exploration.

These operators offer options to explore the island by land or sea, with activities suited to every preference. It's advisable to book ahead, particularly during summer, and check their official websites for promotions or updated details.

For Contacts and Information: Boat Tours and Excursions

To obtain information about excursions and tourist activities in Santorini, you can contact local operators directly. Below are some useful references:

Dakoutros Bros J.V.

- Headquarters: Central Square of Fira, 84700 Santorini, Greece
- Phone: +30 22860 22958 / +30 22860 22686
- Email: info@santorini-excursions.com

Santorini Excursions

- Website: santorini-excursions.com
- Offers boat tours, private excursions, and cultural activities.

Civitatis Santorini

- Provides a wide range of experiences, including boat rides, archaeological excursions, and sunset tours. Book and get support on their website: civitatis.com

Voyage Tips

- Offers suggestions and contacts for guided tours, catamaran trips, and exclusive experiences. Find more details at: voyagetips.com

Every corner of Santorini invites you to explore its unique cultural identity, balancing past and present.

1. Visit Traditional Villages

- **Oia**: Famous for its spectacular sunsets, white houses carved into the rock, and blue-domed churches.
- **Pyrgos**: A picturesque village with cobblestone streets, ancient mansions, and breathtaking panoramic views.

Guided Tours in Pyrgos and Oia

- Local Agency: Santorini Traditions Tours
  Email: info@santorinitraditions.gr
  Phone: +30 22860 12345

2. Explore the Akrotiri Archaeological Site

An ancient Minoan city buried under volcanic ash in 1600 BC. Discover well-preserved frescoes, advanced architecture, and everyday artifacts.

- Tickets and guided tours:
  - Website: hsca.gr
  - Email: akrotiri.info@culture.gr
  - Phone: +30 22860 81490

3. Archaeological Museum and Museum of Prehistoric Thera

- The Archaeological Museum of Fira displays artifacts from the geometric, Hellenistic, and Roman periods.
- The Museum of Prehistoric Thera offers insights into Minoan civilization and the island's evolution.

- Prehistoric Museum - Email: prehistoric.museum@thira.gr;
  ☎+30 22860 23217

- Archaeological Museum - Email: archaeology.museum@thira.grPhone:
  ☎ +30 22860 22217

4. Cultural Festivals and Religious Experiences

- **Ifestia Festival:** An annual celebration of the volcano with fireworks, concerts, and performances.
- **Village Patronal Festivals**: Celebrate with traditional music, dances, and culinary specialties.
- **Visit Byzantine Churches**: Such as the Panagia Episkopi Church in Mesa Gonia and the Orthodox Metropolitan Cathedral in Fira.
- **Monastery of Prophet Elias**: Located at the highest point of the island, offering a blend of spirituality and stunning landscapes.

5. Contemporary and Traditional Art

- **Local Art Galleries**: Like Art Space in Exo Gonia, set in an old wine cellar, showcasing modern and traditional works.
- **Ceramics and Handmade Jewelry**: Workshops offer the chance to create unique pieces.

Art Space Gallery
- Website: artspacesantorini.com
- Email: info@artspacesantorini.com; Phone: +30 22860 327

Santorini's Culture: A Journey Between Tradition and Modernity

Santorini is not only famous for its spectacular sunsets and breathtaking views but also for its rich cultural heritage. The island tells a story spanning millennia, from the ancient Minoan civilization visible at the Akrotiri archaeological site to local traditions preserved in its picturesque villages.

Santorini's culture is reflected in its festivals, religious celebrations, and cuisine, combining authentic flavors and fine wines. Art lovers will find inspiration in local galleries, while those seeking immersive experiences can discover the spirituality of Byzantine churches and island monasteries.

Santorini is a paradise for trekking enthusiasts, offering panoramic trails that combine nature, history, and breathtaking views of the caldera.

1. Fira to Oia Trail

A classic 10 km route, ideal for exploring the beauty of the caldera with picturesque views of villages and the sea.

- Duration: 3-4 hours (moderate level).
- Tip: Start early in the morning or late in the afternoon to avoid the heat.

Local Guides Contacts:
- Santorini Trekking Club - ☎ +30 69445 33421
- Trekking Hellas Cyclades -☎ +30 210 3310323; Email: info@trekking.gr

2. Hike to Cape Columbo

A lesser-known spot, perfect for admiring wild cliffs and the untouched side of the island.

- Duration: 2-3 hours (easy level).
- Starting Point: Parking area near the beach.
- Suggestion: Bring water and sunscreen; there are no nearby facilities.

Contact:
- Santorini Adventure Tours - ☎ +30 69831 25678;
- Email: info@santoriniadventure.com

3. Red Beach Trekking

One of Santorini's most iconic spots, featuring a short but scenic path leading to the famous red beach.

- Duration: 30 minutes (easy level).
- Starting Point: Parking near Akrotiri.

Contacts:
- Kamari Tours (☎ +30 22860 32751; Email:

info@kamaritoursexcursions.gr).

All trails are accessible without a guide, but organized tours offer a deeper experience, including insights into local geology and culture.

For Contacts and Information on Wine and Gastronomic Tastings

To organize a winery tour and discover Santorini's famous volcanic wines, contact the following specialized organizations:

1. Santorini Wine Tour

- **Email**: info@santoriniwinetour.com; **Phone**: +30 698 375 2498
They offer private and semi-private tours of the island's renowned vineyards and wineries, including guided tastings of typical wines like **Assyrtiko** and **Vinsanto**. Thematic tours, such as sunset tastings, are available.

2. Santorini Wine Stories

- Email: info@santoriniwinestories.com
- Phone: +30 690 706 0738
  They provide personalized tours and winery visits, focusing on authentic and educational experiences. Packages may include cooking classes and tastings combined with history and culture.

3. Santo Wines

- Email: reservations@santowines.gr
- Website: santowines.gr
- Phone: +30 22860 22596

4. Estate Argyros Winery

- Email: info@estate-argyros.com
  Located near Pyrgos, this historic winery offers free tastings during less crowded months and visits to Santorini's unique vineyards, ideal for wine enthusiasts.

5. Domaine Sigalas

- Email: info@sigalaswinetasting.com
- Phone: +30 22860 71644
  One of the most acclaimed wineries near Oia, known for Assyrtiko and Mavrotragano tastings and local dishes made with seasonal ingredients.

6. Cooking Classes

- Cooking Santorini
  - Email: cooking@santorini.gr; Phone: +30 22860 55432

For Contacts and Information on Water Sports and Outdoor Activities

Santorini offers numerous opportunities for sports and adventure enthusiasts, both on water and land.

1. **Snorkeling and Diving**: Explore volcanic seabeds and underwater caves with unique marine life. Major centers include:

   ○ Santorini Dive Center (Akrotiri, ☎ +30 22860 81400)

   ○ Aegean Divers (Fira, ☎ +30 22860 33215)

2. **Kitesurfing and Windsurfing**: Ideal in Monolithos Bay due to constant winds. Contact:

   ○ Santorini Kite (Monolithos, ☎ +30 69744 22334)

3. **Kayaking and Paddleboarding**: Perfect for exploring the rugged coastline and secluded beaches. Guided tours available:

   ○ Santorini Sea Kayak (Mesa Pigadia, ☎ +30 69727 68258)

   ○ Caldera SUP (Perissa, ☎ +30 69872 12245)

All activities are managed by professionals and suitable for all experience levels.

5. ACCOMMODATIONS AND RESTAURANTS

Santorini: One Island, Endless Possibilities

Santorini offers a wide range of accommodations for every need and budget, all with a unique charm. From luxury suites with infinity pools overlooking the caldera to mid-range boutique hotels, budget accommodations, and traditional cave houses, every option promises an unforgettable stay. Whether you seek romance, adventure, or relaxation, the island guarantees a welcoming atmosphere and breathtaking views.

5.1 Luxury Hotels (Average price: €600–€1200 per night)

1. Katikies Hotel (Oia)

- **Description**: A luxury icon in Santorini, combining Cycladic architecture and modern comforts. Features suites with private terraces and infinity pools overlooking the caldera, ideal for honeymoons or romantic escapes.
- **Main Amenities**: Gourmet restaurant, spa, dedicated concierge service.
- **Highlights**: Central location in Oia, perfect for sunset walks. Unforgettable infinity pool with caldera views.

Website: katikies.com; Phone: ☎ +30 22860 71401

2. Grace Hotel Santorini (Imerovigli)

- **Description**: Part of Auberge Resorts, blending modern minimalism with Greek warmth. Suites include hot tubs and private infinity pools.
- **Main Amenities**: Champagne lounge, outdoor yoga, personalized private dining.
- **Highlights**: Unique à la carte gourmet breakfast. Maximum privacy in suites with infinity pools.

Website: aubergeresorts.com/gracehotel; ☎ +30 22860 21300

3. Canaves Oia Suites & Spa (Oia)

- ○ **Description**: Sophisticated and scenic, offering privacy and luxury. Exclusive spa treatments and elegantly designed suites.
- ○ **Main Amenities**: Private yacht excursions, wine tastings, 24-hour room service.
- ○ **Highlights**: Private dining with caldera views. Exceptional spa services.

Website: canaves.com; ☎ +30 22860 71453

5.2 Mid-Range Hotels (Average price: €200-€400 per night)

1. Astra Suites (Imerovigli)

- ○ **Description:** Perched on a cliff, it is renowned for its intimate atmosphere and breathtaking views. It offers spacious suites with kitchenettes and private balconies.
- ○ **Main Amenities:** Caldera-view pool, in-room breakfast service, shuttle service.
- ○ **Highlights:** The pool with caldera-view loungers is perfect for relaxation. The staff is very helpful in organizing tours.

Website: astrasuites.com; ☎ +30 22860 71401

2. Petit Palace Suites (Fira)

- ○ **Description:** Located a short distance from Fira's center, Petit Palace combines a boutique atmosphere with a strategic position for exploring the island.
- ○ **Main Amenities:** Infinity pool, restaurant with a view, car and bike rentals.
- ○ **Highlights:** Infinity pool and free shuttle service to Fira center.

Website: petitepalace.gr; ☎ +30 22860 25870

3. Santorini Secret Premium (Oia)

- ○ **Description:** A modern hotel with traditional Cycladic design, offering elegant suites with attention to detail.
  Main Amenities: Private hot tubs, local cuisine restaurant, concierge service.

- o **Highlights:** Outdoor private hot tubs for every suite and personalized breakfast.

Website: santorinisecret.com; ☎ +30 22860 27336

5.3 Budget Hotels (Average price: €80-€150 per night)

1. Anemomilos Hotel (Oia)

- o **Description:** Cozy and simple, the hotel is just a short walk from Oia's center. Perfect for those seeking an affordable stay close to major attractions.
- o **Main Amenities:** Pool, Greek cuisine restaurant, free parking.
- o **Highlights:** Large pool and on-site restaurant offering traditional Greek dishes at moderate prices.

Website: anemomilos.com; ☎ +30 22860 71410

2. Villa Manos (Karterados)

- o **Description:** Ideal for families and groups, this property offers a wide range of rooms and apartments with a friendly, family-run atmosphere.
- o **Main Amenities:** Large pool with bar, equipped kitchen, transfers upon request.
- o **Highlights:** Quiet location close to Fira, and excellent pool facilities.

Website: villamanos.gr; ☎ +30 22860 25627

3. Hotel Lignos (Fira)

- o **Description:** Situated in the heart of Fira, it's perfect for travelers seeking budget-friendly accommodation with convenient access to shops, restaurants, and public transport.
- o **Main Amenities:** Free Wi-Fi, 24-hour reception, luggage storage.
- o **Highlights:** Competitive pricing and free Wi-Fi throughout the property.

Website: lignos-santorini.com; ☎ +30 22860 22768

5.4 Holiday Homes and Affordable Options

1. Alexander's Boutique Hotel (Oia) (Mid-range €150-€250 per night)

- o **Description:** Traditional cave houses with authentic decor and kitchenettes, ideal for families or small groups.
- o **Main Amenities:** Panoramic terrace, equipped kitchen, laundry service upon request.
- o **Highlights:** Kitchenettes and private terraces in most houses. Perfect for families.

Website: alexandershotel.com; ☎ +30 22860 71818

2. Santorini Caves (Emporio) - (from €100)

- o **Description:** Located in a less touristy village, it offers unique accommodations in traditional Santorini cave houses. Great for an authentic experience.
- o **Main Amenities:** Free Wi-Fi, shared kitchen, scooter rental.
- o **Highlights:** Authentic location away from the crowds but well-connected to major attractions.

Website: santocaves.com; ☎ +30 694 920 8430

3. Blue Dolphin Apartments (Kamari) - (from €80 per night)

- o **Description:** Just a short walk from Kamari Beach, this property is ideal for those looking to relax by the sea without overspending.
- o **Main Amenities:** Air-conditioned rooms, pool, barbecue area.
- o **Highlights:** Barbecue area and bike rental options.

Website: dolphins-santorini.gr; ☎ +30 22860 31302

4. Airbnb and Local Options (from €50 per night)

- o **Description:** Numerous apartments and studios are available in less crowded locations like Perissa, Emporio, and Akrotiri. Many offer fully equipped kitchens and private outdoor spaces.
- o **Highlights:** Wide availability of affordable solutions and apartments for groups.

5.5 Fine Dining Restaurants

1. Selene (Pyrgos)

- o **Description**: A true icon of the island's haute cuisine, Selene offers sophisticated dishes that reinterpret Greek tradition with local ingredients. The location is elegant and boasts panoramic views.
- o **Average price**: €100–€150 per person.
- o **Tips**: Reservation is mandatory; perfect for a special evening.

Address/Phone: Pyrgos, Santorini 8470; ☎ +30 22860 22249

2. Lauda Restaurant (Oia)

- o **Description:** Located in a privileged spot in Oia, this Michelin-starred restaurant offers creative cuisine with breathtaking views of the caldera.
- o **Average price:** €120–€200 per person.
- o **Tips:** Perfect for sunset tastings. The tasting menu is highly recommended.

Address/Phone: Andronis Boutique Hotel, Oia, Santorini 84702;
☎ +30 22860 72077

3. Ambrosia (Oia)

- o **Description:** A romantic atmosphere paired with gourmet cuisine. The menu includes carefully reimagined Mediterranean dishes and an excellent wine selection.
- o **Average price:** €90–€130 per person.
- o **Tips:** Ask for a terrace table to enjoy enchanting views.

Address/Phone: Oia Main Street, Santorini 84702; ☎ +30 22860 71413

5.6 Traditional Restaurants and Taverns

1. Metaxy Mas (Exo Gonia)

- o **Description:** One of the most beloved taverns, famous for its traditional dishes and welcoming atmosphere. The menu features a wide range of Cretan and Santorini specialties.
- o **Average price**: €25–€40 per person.

- o **Tips:** Ideal for those seeking an authentic Greek experience. Reservation recommended.

Address/Phone: Exo Gonia, Santorini 84700; ☎ +30 22860 31323

2. Karma (Oia)

- o **Description:** This restaurant stands out for its Cycladic decor and a menu that combines local recipes with a modern twist.
- o **Average price:** €30–€50 per person.
- o **Tips:** Great for a relaxed lunch in the center of Oia.

Address/Phone: Main Street, Oia, Santorini 84702; ☎ +30 22860 71815

3. Taverna To Psaraki (Vlychada)

- o **Description:** Specializing in fresh fish, this tavern is renowned for the simplicity and quality of its dishes, with views of the harbor.
- o **Average price:** €20–€40 per person.
- o **Tips:** Try the grilled calamari and the daily specials.

Address/Phone: Vlychada Marina, Santorini 84700; ☎ +30 22860 82783

4. Roka (Oia)

- o **Description:** A hidden gem in the heart of Oia, known for its intimate atmosphere and creatively reimagined traditional dishes.
- o **Average price:** €25–€40 per person.
- o **Tips:** Don't miss the daily specials and the salad with local capers.

Address/Phone: Epar.Od. Firon-Ias, Oia, Santorini 84702;
☎ +30 22860 71869

5. The Good Heart (Akrotiri)

- o **Description:** A family-run tavern serving authentic local recipes made with home-grown ingredients. Perfect for a genuine experience.
- o **Average price:** €20–€35 per person.
- o **Tips:** Arrive early to secure a table, especially during peak season. Try the daily specials.

Address/Phone: Akrotiri, Santorini 84700; ☎ +30 22860 82016

5.7 Budget-friendly Options

1. Lucky's Souvlaki (Fira)

- **Description:** One of the best spots to enjoy classic souvlaki at unbeatable prices. Perfect for quick meals.
- **Average price:** €5–€10 per person.
- **Tips:** Ideal for a snack between visits.

Address/Phone: Danezi M, Fira, Santorini 84700; ☎ +30 22860 22003

2. Pitogyros (Oia)

- **Description:** Famous for its gyros, offering tasty and abundant dishes in a casual setting.
- **Average price:** €10–€15 per person.
- **Tips:** Great for families or groups of friends seeking a quick meal.

Address/Phone: Oia Main Street, Santorini 84702; ☎ +30 22860 71888

3. Falafel Land (Fira)

- **Description:** Specializes in vegetarian and vegan options. Fresh and flavorful falafel served with hummus and salads.
- **Average price:** €8–€12 per person.
- **Tips**: Perfect for a light and healthy lunch break.

Address/Phone: Dekigala, Fira, Santorini 84700; ☎ +30 22860 21824

4. Nick the Grill (Perissa)

- **Description:** A casual spot serving quality gyros and souvlaki at reasonable prices, just steps from the beach.
- **Average price:** €10–€15 per person.
  Tips: Great for a quick lunch after a morning at the beach. The chicken gyros is especially popular.

Address/Phone: Main Road, Perissa, Santorini 84703; ☎ +30 22860 85188

5. Taverna Santa Irini (Perivolos)

- **Description:** A cozy little tavern, ideal for budget-friendly snacks and fresh salads by the sea.
- **Average price:** €12–€18 per person.

- Tips: Perfect for a light meal with a sea view. Portions are
  generous.
  Address/Phone: Perivolos Beach, Santorini 84703; ☎ +30 22860 8255

> ➡ **Reservations:** In fine dining restaurants and popular tavernas, it is
> recommended to book in advance, especially during the high season.
>
> ➡ **Payment Policies:** Some restaurants accept cash only; check in advance.

Whether it's a meal in a traditional taverna with a view of the caldera, a wine tasting in a historic winery, or a creative dish served in a gourmet restaurant, Santorini's cuisine will leave you with unforgettable memories.

5.8 Best Seafood Restaurants in Santorini

Santorini offers a variety of seafood restaurants, ranging from small family-run establishments to more elegant and refined venues, all sharing a commitment to high-quality local seafood. Here is a selection of restaurants where you can savor the best fish on the island.

1. Taverna Katina (Amoudi Bay)

- **Address:** Amoudi Bay, Oia, Santorini
- **Phone:** +30 22860 71614
- **Specialties:** Grilled octopus, fried calamari, kakavia.
- **Description:** One of the most famous taverns in Santorini, located at Amoudi Bay, where you can dine right on the beach with spectacular sea views. The fish is freshly caught by local fishermen.
- **Price range:** Medium, around €20–€40 per person.
- **Tip**: Arrive early or book a table near the sea; the atmosphere at sunset is magical.

2. Astra Restaurant (Imerovigli)

- **Address:** Imerovigli, Santorini 84700
- **Phone:** +30 22860 23641
- **Specialties:** Baked sea bream, sea urchins, grilled grouper.
- **Description:** An elegant restaurant with breathtaking views of the caldera. Perfect for a romantic dinner, serving refined fresh fish dishes.
- **Price range:** High, around €50–€70 per person.
- **Tip:** Ideal for couples; request a table with a caldera view for an unforgettable evening.

3. Seaside by Notos (Perivolos)

- **Address:** Perivolos Beach, Santorini
- **Phone:** +30 22860 82801
- **Specialties:** Fresh fish sushi, grilled octopus, sea urchin salad.
- **Description:** An elegant restaurant on Perivolos Beach, perfect for dining with your feet in the sand. Offers a wide selection of fresh fish and creative dishes.

- **Price range:** Medium, around €30–€50 per person.
- **Tip:** Visit in the late afternoon for a relaxed lunch followed by a swim.

4. To Psaraki (Vlychada)

- **Address:** Vlychada Marina, Santorini
- **Phone:** +30 22860 82783
- **Specialties:** Grilled fresh fish, baked fish, shrimp saganaki (with feta and tomato).
- **Description:** Renowned for its fresh fish and simple yet delicious dishes in a tranquil atmosphere. Located near Vlychada port, perfect for an authentic meal.
- **Price range:** Medium, around €25–€45 per person.
  Tip: Try the recommended daily specials; they often feature the best local catches.

6. The Cuisine of Santorini: An Explosion of Unique Flavors

The gastronomy of Santorini reflects the island's unique character, shaped by its volcanic soil, Mediterranean sun, and Aegean winds. Every dish tells a story tied to local traditions and the resilience of a generous land that overcomes natural challenges, making a trip to Santorini unforgettable for the palate.

Introduction to Santorini's Cuisine

Santorini's cuisine is a sensory journey blending authentic flavors, local ingredients, and a culinary tradition rooted in the Cyclades' culture. This small volcanic island not only enchants with breathtaking landscapes but also offers visitors a unique gastronomic experience shaped by its history, geography, and connection to the sea.

The soil of Santorini, rich in minerals due to volcanic activity, is the perfect habitat for unique crops, such as the island's famous small and sweet cherry tomatoes and fava beans, a local legume variety with a delicate flavor. Wine also plays a starring role: the island's vineyards, cultivated using the traditional "basket" method to protect them from strong winds and intense sun, produce globally renowned wines like Assyrtiko and Vinsanto.

In addition to the land's bounty, Santorini's cuisine thrives on the riches of the Aegean Sea. Fresh fish, shellfish, and mollusks form the basis of many traditional dishes, often prepared simply to highlight the quality of the raw ingredients. This symbiotic relationship between land and sea is reflected in an essential yet flavorful cuisine that celebrates the authenticity of its ingredients.

6.1 Fishing in Santorini

Fishing has a long-standing tradition in Santorini, dating back to antiquity. Thanks to its location in the heart of the Aegean Sea, the island has always been a prime destination for fishermen. The crystal-clear waters and the variety of marine species surrounding the island make fishing a key activity, not only for local subsistence but also for the gastronomic culture of Santorini.

In Santorini, fishing is both a historical tradition and a vital economic activity. The island's fishermen continue to use traditional methods, passed down through generations, to catch fresh fish and seafood. Today, in addition to supplying local restaurants, fishing has also become a tourist attraction, offering experiences such as a day at sea or enjoying freshly caught fish straight from the surrounding waters.

Fishing in Santorini is more than a commercial activity; it is a central element of the island's gastronomic culture. Fresh fish is one of the main ingredients in local cuisine, renowned for its simplicity and the quality of its products. In the island's restaurants and taverns, fish-based dishes are an essential part of the culinary tradition, making fishing not just a livelihood but a cultural experience for visitors.

Types of Fish Caught in Santorini

Santorini's strategic position in the Aegean Sea makes its waters rich in a variety of fish and seafood. Some of the main species caught on the island include:

- **Sea Bream and Sea Bass:** Highly prized for their tender and flavorful meat, often served grilled or baked.

- **Dentex and Grouper:** Bottom-dwelling fish commonly featured in fish soups or as main courses.

- **Squid and Octopus:** Frequently used in local dishes, whether fried, grilled, or as marinated appetizers.

- **Anchovies and Sardines:** Small bluefish, served fresh or preserved in salt.

- **Scorpionfish and Gurnard:** Often used to prepare "kakavia," the traditional Greek fish soup.

- **Sea Urchins:** Hand-harvested by divers, these are considered a delicacy and are served fresh with olive oil and lemon.

6.2 Fishing Bans and Seasonality

Fishing in Santorini follows specific regulations to ensure the sustainability of marine resources and preserve the Aegean Sea's ecosystem.

Seasonal Fishing Bans:

Certain types of fishing are prohibited during specific times of the year to allow species to reproduce. For example:

- **Octopus:** Fishing is banned from May to June during the breeding season.
- **Sea Urchins:** Harvesting is usually prohibited from mid-April to late May.
- **Bottom Fish (Grouper, Dentex):** Fishing is regulated during winter, their breeding season.

Seasonality of the Catch:

The availability of fish varies throughout the year. Some examples include:

- **Spring:** Squid and sardines are abundant.

- **Summer:** Octopus, sea bream, and sea bass dominate the menu

- **Autumn:** The ideal season for shellfish and a wider variety of fish.

- **Winter:** Fish soups and stews featuring scorpionfish and gurnard are popular choices.

Fishing is primarily conducted off the southern coast, in deeper waters where the best catches can be found.

Traditional Fishing Techniques

In Santorini, fishing has been practiced for centuries, and many traditional techniques are still in use, passed down from generation to generation. Here are the most common ones:

- **Gill Nets (Kalamaria)**
  One of the most widely used methods by local fishermen. The nets are placed on the seabed overnight and retrieved in the morning. This technique is ideal for catching fish such as sea bream, sea bass, and dentex.

- **Longlines (Palamiti)**
  A long fishing line equipped with numerous baited hooks, used to catch larger fish such as groupers and tuna. Experienced fishermen know the best spots to position the lines, often far from tourist areas.

- **Trap Fishing**
  Funnel-shaped baskets made of wood or metal, used to trap crustaceans and octopuses. This method is environmentally friendly, as the traps allow for the easy release of unwanted specimens

- **Spearfishing**
  Popular for harvesting sea urchins and octopuses, this technique requires skill and experience. Divers use handheld spears to capture their prey.

- **Coastal Trolling**
  A traditional method where a boat tows moving fishing lines to attract pelagic species like tuna and mackerel.

These techniques are often carried out at dawn or dusk when the waters are calmer, and fish are more likely to approach the shore. Additionally, many fishing families sell their daily catch directly at small ports like Ammoudi, offering visitors an authentic experience.

6.3 Local Fish in Santorini's Restaurants

Santorini is a paradise for lovers of fresh fish, and its restaurants offer the best locally caught seafood. Fish-based dishes are a fundamental part of the island's cuisine, often prepared with fresh and simple ingredients to highlight the taste of the sea.

Typical Fish Found in Restaurants:
- **Sea Bream:** Delicate and flavorful, often baked or grilled.
- **Octopus and Squid:** Prepared in various ways, from simple grilling to more elaborate stews.
- **Dentex and Grouper:** Popular in soups or served whole and baked.
- **Sea Urchins:** Highly sought after in spring, served fresh straight from the local waters.

Signature Fish Dishes:
- **Kakavia:** Traditional Greek fish soup, made with a selection of fresh fish, vegetables, and broth. It is a hearty and flavorful dish, perfect for cooler days.
- **Grilled Octopus:** Freshly caught octopus is often grilled and served with a drizzle of olive oil, lemon, and local herbs.

- **Fried Squid (Soutzouk Loukoum):** Fresh squid, breaded and fried, served as an appetizer or main course.
- **Fish en Papillote:** Local fish like sea bream or sea bass cooked in parchment paper with fresh herbs and tomatoes.

6.4 Typical Products: The Heart of Local Cuisine

The island's gastronomy is not just a pleasure for the palate but also a cultural journey. Every dish tells a story, intertwining Byzantine, Venetian, and Ottoman influences, showcasing the resilience of Santorini's inhabitants, who transformed an apparently barren land into a source of unforgettable flavors.

Santorini Fava Beans:

This legume, similar to a small yellow lentil, has been cultivated on the island for over 3,500 years. Made into a velvety puree, fava is served with olive oil, onions, capers, and sometimes a squeeze of lemon. It is a symbol of the island and recognized as a PDO product.

Santorini Capers:

With their intense, slightly salty, and tangy flavor, capers and their leaves are a key ingredient in local salads and fish dishes. Hand-harvested, they grow wild among volcanic rocks, absorbing the minerals that enhance their taste

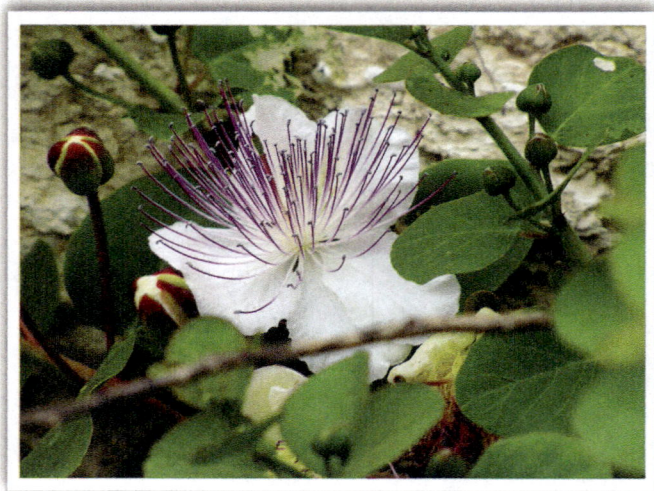

Santorini Cherry Tomatoes:

These small tomatoes, with their sweet and intense flavor, thrive thanks to the unique combination of wind, sun, and volcanic soil. They are used to make the famous tomatokeftedes (fried tomato balls) and traditional sauces.

White Eggplants:

A unique variety of eggplant, characterized by its pale skin and seedless, creamy flesh, often grilled, fried, or used in traditional dishes like moussaka. Grown in Santorini's volcanic soil, they absorb less water than common eggplants, resulting in a firmer and more flavorful texture.

Volcanic Wines: The Excellence of Santorini

Santorini is renowned for its fine wines, thanks to the unique volcanic terrain and the traditional *kouloura* cultivation method, where vines are grown in basket shapes to protect the grapes from the wind.

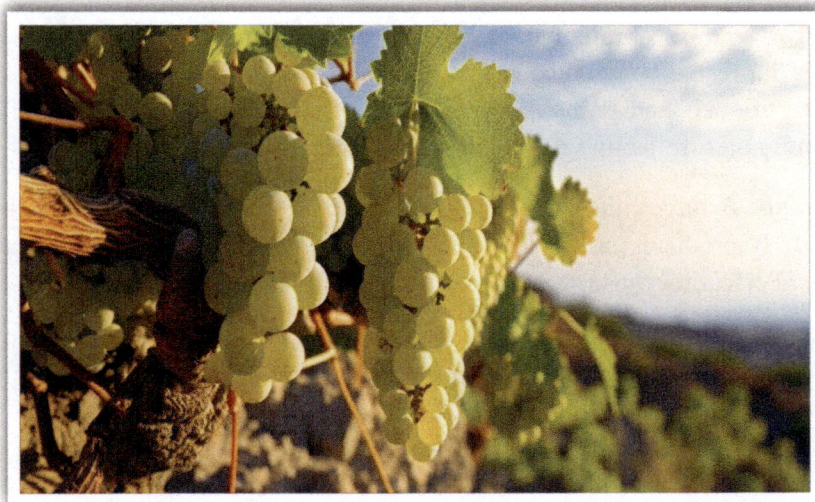

1. **Assyrtiko:** This dry white wine is the jewel of local winemaking. Fresh, mineral, and with a slight acidity, it pairs perfectly with seafood dishes and Mediterranean flavors. It maintains a robust structure and excellent aging potential, offering complex nuances over time, with hints of honey, toasted almonds, and beeswax.

2. **Vinsanto:** A sweet wine made from Assyrtiko grapes, with small amounts of Aidani and Athiri, sun-dried to concentrate sugars and aromas. Aged in wooden barrels, it features notes of honey, dried fruit, and caramel. It is a traditional wine, often served at the end of a meal or with local desserts.

3. **Nykteri:** A full-bodied and aromatic white wine, produced from grapes harvested at night (nykteri in Greek), to preserve their freshness.

4. **Athiri:** An indigenous grape variety often used in blends with Assyrtiko. It produces fresh, light, and aromatic white wines, with fruity and floral notes. Ideal for those seeking softer and more delicate wines, perfect for aperitifs and light dishes.

5. **Aidani:** Another typical Santorini white grape, characterized by floral aromas and a soft taste. It is often used to sweeten dry wines such as Nykteri or to add complexity to Vinsanto.

6. **Mavrotragano:** A rare red grape variety, traditionally used for sweet wines but recently reevaluated for the production of dry red wines. These wines are rich and complex, with hints of ripe red fruits, spices, and mineral notes, reflecting the volcanic character of the island.

7. **Katsano:** A rare white grape variety grown in limited quantities on the island. It produces aromatic wines with notes of honey, flowers, and citrus. Perfect for those seeking a unique and authentic wine experience.

8. **Mezzo:** A semi-sweet wine typical of Cycladic tradition. It can be made from Assyrtiko, Aidani, or other local grapes and pairs wonderfully with slightly sweet or spicy dishes.

Traditional Dishes Not to Miss

1. **Tomatokefdes**: Tomato fritters with onion, herbs, and flour, fried until crispy.
2. **Sfougato**: A frittata with zucchini, potatoes, fresh herbs, and local cheese.
3. **Atherinopita**: A savory pie with small fried fish, typical of coastal tavernas.
4. **Kopania**: Sweets made from carob flour and sesame, perfect for a sweet break.
5. **Chlorotyri:** A fresh and soft cheese typical of Santorini, with a slightly tangy flavor. Perfect as an appetizer or paired with local bread and cherry tomatoes.
6. **Kserotigana:** Crispy, fried pastries shaped into spirals, drizzled with honey and topped with nuts. Often served during weddings or festivities, they are a true traditional treat.

7. Practical Tips for Visiting Santorini

Organizing your visit to Santorini is essential to fully enjoy its beauty and have a stress-free experience. Here's a practical guide with everything you need to know about transportation, rentals, and behavior on the island.

7.1 Car, Scooter, and Boat Rentals

Why rent them: Santorini is an island with narrow roads and breathtaking landscapes, and having your own vehicle allows you to easily reach beaches, villages, and attractions.

Where to rent: Numerous local agencies offer cars and scooters, available at the airport or the Athinios port. Some of the most reliable are:

- *Motor Inn Santorini* (office at the airport - tel. +30 22860 21685 - website: motorinn.gr)

- *Santorini Rent a Car* (at the airport and Athinios port) tel. +30 697 343 6690 - website: autorent-santorini.com

▷ **Car**: €40–€100 per day (depending on model and season).

▷ **Scooter**: €15–€40 per day.

Tips:

▷ Make sure you have a valid driving license (for scooters, a motorcycle license is often required).

▷ Book in advance during high season to secure the best price.

Boat Rentals

An unforgettable experience: Exploring Santorini by sea lets you discover hidden bays, hot springs, and spectacular views of the caldera.

Boat rental agencies:

- Karolos Boat Rentals, at Vlichada port; tel. +30 693 668 7788; Email: info@karolosrentalboats.com
- Santo Boats, at Extreme Watersports, near Perivolos beach; tel. +30 698 739 8306; Email: hello@santoboats.com
- Alex Boat Tours, at the Old Port under Fira; tel. +30 2286083013; +30 6972331040; Email: joyalex@otenet.gr

Available Options:

- Boats without a license: Ideal for beginners, available for half a day or a full day (€150–€300).
- Guided tours or private yachts: Starting from €100 per person.

Tips:

- Bring sunscreen and water.
- Check weather conditions before departing.

7.2 Public and Private Transportation

Public Transport

▷ **KTEL Buses**

Local buses are the most economical way to get around. Main routes connect Fira (the transportation hub) with Oia, Perissa, Kamari, and Akrotiri.
Prices: From €1.80 to €2.50 per ride.
Timetable: During high season, buses run until midnight, but frequency may decrease in the evening.

Taxis and Private Transfers

▷ **Taxis**

Limited on the island and often hard to find during high season. It's advisable to book in advance.
Average cost: €25–€40 for a short ride (e.g., from Fira to Oia).

Private Transfers

Offered by many agencies, they are a great option for comfort and punctuality. Prices start at €30 per ride for two people.

7.3 Gas Station Opening Hours

Standard Hours:

▷ Gas stations are open from 7:00 AM to 9:00 PM, but during high season, some remain open until midnight.

▷ The main stations are along the main roads between Fira, Kamari, and Perissa.

Tip: If you rent a scooter or car, fill up during the central hours of the day to avoid unexpected issues.

7.4 What to Do and What to Avoid in Santorini

What to Do

- **Plan ahead:** Santorini is very popular, so book hotels, restaurants, and activities well in advance during high season.
- **Follow the road code**: The island's roads are narrow and often crowded. Drive carefully and use designated parking.
- **Explore less-known villages:** Pyrgos, Megalochori, and Emporio offer an authentic atmosphere away from the crowds of Oia and Fira.
- **Witness the sunrise:** While Oia's sunset is iconic, the sunrise from the eastern side of the island is equally spectacular and less crowded.

What to Avoid

- **Don't use donkeys as transportation:** While it's a tradition, responsible tourism discourages this practice.
- **Don't wait until the last minute to book:** From transportation to restaurants, availability is limited.
- **Don't leave trash:** Santorini is a natural paradise, so keep beaches and trails clean to preserve its beauty.
- Don't neglect sun protection: The sun in Santorini can be very intense, especially in summer. Sunscreen, a hat, and a water bottle are essential to enjoy the island safely.
- **Don't drive without experience on winding roads:** The roads in Santorini, particularly those along the caldera, can be challenging and narrow. If you're not an experienced driver, consider alternatives like buses, taxis, or ATVs to get around safely.

8. MAP OF THE ISLAND AND RECOMMENDED ITINERARIES

A trip to Santorini deserves careful planning to fully enjoy its natural, cultural, and gastronomic beauties. The island, with its unique crescent

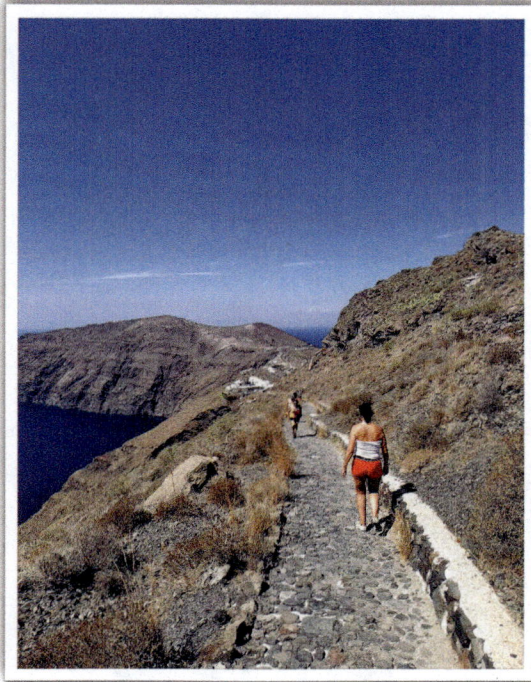

shape, invites exploration of every hidden corner, from picturesque villages on the cliffs to archaeological sites rich in history. Thanks to its volcanic nature, each beach offers a different experience: from the red sands of Red Beach to the black pebbles of Kamari, to the lunar calm of Vlychada. Get lost in the breathtaking views where the blue of the sea meets the bright white of the Cycladic houses.

Planning your itinerary is essential to ensure you make the most of this unique destination. In the map below, you'll find the main points of interest, like Fira, the island's vibrant capital, and Oia, famous for the most photographed sunsets in the world. If you have limited time, follow the **three-day itinerary**: it will guide you through unmissable attractions, balancing culture, relaxation, and culinary delights. If you have more time, the extended **five-day itinerary** will allow you to explore every corner of the island, including hiking trails like the famous route from Fira to Oia, offering unmatched panoramic views.

1 • Aghios Nikolaos
2 • Stairsto Ammoudi Beach
3 • Oia Goulas (castle ruins)
4 • Mavro Vouno summit 329m
5 • Island's narrowest point (canteen)
6 • Aghios Antonios-Neos (church & taskitarion)
7 • Imerovigli cemetery
8 • Panaghia Malteza church
9 • Aghios Nikolaos Monastery
10 • Dominican Monastery, Megaron Gizi Museum
11 • Stairsto Fira port
12 • Fira Health Center (First Aid Station)
13 • Fira mines
14 • Akrotiri mines
15 • Akrotiri windmill
16 • Junction of footpath
17 • Panaghia Kimisis church
18 • Ftelou Square
19 • Taxiarchis church
20 • Akrotiri excavations
21 • Aghia Anna church
22 • Emporio windmills
23 • Stairsto Vlichada beach
24 • Ancient Elefsina
25 • Ancient Elefsina ruins
26 • Profitis Ilias Monastery
27 • Ancient Thira (Entrance to excavations)
28 • Old tomato paste factory
29 • Aghios Ioannis Monastery
30 • Karterados sandy road
31 • Pori
32 • Arched graves
33 • Tholos
34 • Panaghia Episkopi Byzantine church
35 • Pyrgos castle
36 • Emporio Goulas (castle ruins)
37 • Small cave with fortifications

To enlarge the map ⇨

SCAN ME

Map of Santorini

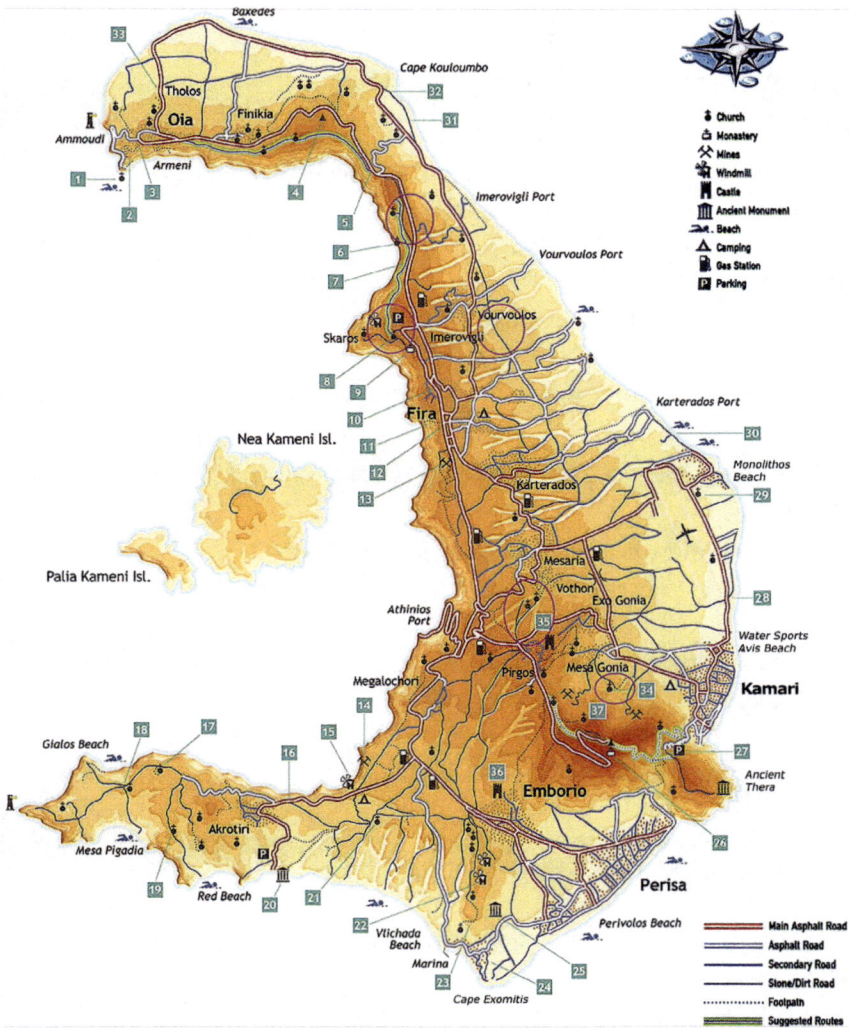

Baxedes

Cape Kouloumbo

33

Tholos

Oia

Finikia

32

31

Ammoudi

Armeni

Imerovigli Port

1

3

4

2

5

Vourvoulos Port

6

7

Skaros

Yourvoulos

Karterados Port

Imerovigli

8

9

Fira

30

10

Nea Kameni Isl.

11

Monolithos Beach

12

Karterados

29

13

Mesaria

Palia Kameni Isl.

Vothon

Exo Gonia

28

Athinios Port

35

Water Sports Avis Beach

Megalochori

Pirgos

Mesa Gonia

Kamari

14

34

Gialos Beach

18

17

15

37

16

36

Emborio

27

Ancient Thera

Akrotiri

Mesa Pigadia

26

Perisa

19

Red Beach

20

21

Vlichada Beach

22

Perivolos Beach

Marina

25

23

24

Cape Exomitis

Legend

- Church
- Monastery
- Mines
- Windmill
- Castle
- Ancient Monument
- Beach
- Camping
- Gas Station
- Parking

- Main Asphalt Road
- Asphalt Road
- Secondary Road
- Stone/Dirt Road
- Footpath
- Suggested Routes

8.1 Suggested Itinerary: 3 Days in Santorini

Perfect for a taste of the island, ideal for those who want to combine relaxation and discovery.

Day 1: Welcome to Santorini

▷ *Morning:*
- Explore Fira, visit the Museum of Prehistory to learn about the island's history.
- Take a walk to Firostefani and Imerovigli along the scenic path.

▷ **Afternoon:**
- Relax at a beach like Kamari or Perissa.

▷ *Evening*
- ***Dinner in Oia and watch the sunset from the Fortress.***

Day 2: Discovering History and the Sea

▷ *Morning*:
- Visit Akrotiri, the Minoan archaeological site.
- Explore the nearby Red Beach.

▷ *Afternoon*:
- Take a caldera cruise, with a visit to the hot springs and the Nea Kameni volcano.

▷ *Evening*:
- Dinner in a traditional taverna in Akrotiri.

Day 3: Traditions and Views

▷ *Morning*:
- Explore Pyrgos, a traditional village with spectacular views of the island.

▷ *Afternoon*:
- Visit a winery for a taste of local wines.

▷ *Evening*:
- Dinner in a taverna with a view of the caldera in Firostefani.

8.2 Suggested Itinerary: 5 Days in Santorini

Ideal for a more complete and relaxed experience.

Day 1 & 2: Follow the 3-day itinerary.

Day 3: Beaches and the Sea

Spend the entire day at the beaches:

▷ *Morning:*
  - Perivolos Beach with its crystal-clear waters.
▷ *Afternoon*:
  - Vlychada Beach, famous for its rock formations.
▷ *Evening*:
  - Aperitif and dinner on the beach.

Day 4: Villages and Traditions

▷ *Morning*:
  - Explore Megalochori and its picturesque streets.
▷ *Afternoon*:
  - Hike to Emporio, with its medieval ruins.
▷ *Evening*:
  - Enjoy dinner at a taverna in Pyrgos.

Day 5: Immersion in Nature

▷ *Morning*:
  - A panoramic walk from Fira to Oia along the coastal path (approximately 3 hours).
▷ *Afternoon*:
  - Relax with a massage or spa treatment.
▷ *Evening*:
  - Celebrate the end of the trip with a sunset cruise.

9. The Magic of the Night in Santorini:
Bars, Clubs, and Fun Under the Stars

When the sun sets on the caldera and the sky fills with stars, Santorini transforms into an enchanted island, ready to offer you unforgettable evenings. The nightlife here is an irresistible mix of elegance, emotions, and vibes that will keep you going until dawn. Whether you want to relax with a cocktail in hand, admiring one of the most stunning views in the world, or let yourself be swept away by the rhythm of the music, Santorini will captivate you.

9.1 Cocktails with a View: Sunsets to Sip

Imagine yourself on a panoramic terrace, with the sea breeze caressing your face and a perfectly shaken cocktail in your hand. Here's what awaits you in Santorini's panoramic bars.

- **PK Cocktail Bar (Fira)**: Choose a front-row seat, order a "Santorini Sunrise" and let yourself be mesmerized by the view that stretches to the horizon. Every sip is a tribute to the island's beauty.

- **Franco's Bar (Fira)**: Here, the magic is in the details: classical music playing in the background, soft lighting, and an atmosphere that invites you to dream.

- **Bar Nighteo (Imerovigli)**: A small corner of paradise, where signature cocktails and breathtaking landscapes come together in a unique experience.

Live Music: Heart and Soul of the Evening

If you prefer a more relaxed, yet no less captivating, atmosphere, live music venues are your ideal place.

- **Jazz Bar Kira Thira (Fira)**: Enter and let yourself be enveloped by the warmth of this historic venue. Jazz notes fill the air while the decorated walls tell stories of memorable evenings.

- **Volkan on the Rocks (Firostefani)**: With the caldera in the background and live performances ranging from folk to world music, this venue is a celebration of Greek culture and the good life.

9.2 Nightclubs and Clubs: Pure Energy Under the Stars

For those who love to dance until dawn, Santorini offers a lively, sparkling side that never disappoints.

- **Enigma Club (Fira)**: Get ready to step into a world of lights, sounds, and vibes. Here, the dance floor is the heartbeat of the night.
- **Koo Club (Fira)**: A mix of elegance and fun, with an outdoor garden to relax before returning to the dance floor.
- **Mamounia Club (Fira)**: If you want to experience an authentically Greek evening, this is the place to be. Traditional music blends with international pop, creating a unique atmosphere.

Special Events: Unforgettable Nights

The summer in Santorini is dotted with events that make every night unique. From exclusive parties at beach clubs to sunset cocktail parties organized in luxury hotels, every corner of the island offers opportunities to celebrate life. Don't miss the themed evenings at Canaves Oia Suites or the DJ sets at the venues in Kamari.

Tips for a Perfect Night

- **Getting around the island**: Taxis are the most practical option for getting around at night, especially if you plan to enjoy a couple of drinks.

- **The right outfit**: Go for a casual-chic look, perfect for moving from the bar to the club. Don't forget comfortable shoes for walking on the cobbled streets!

- **Timing**: Bars start to fill up as soon as the sun sets, while the clubs come alive after midnight.

Don't rush: The night in Santorini is long and full of surprises.

10. Shopping in Santorini

Shopping in Santorini is a unique experience, combining the pleasure of buying with the discovery of local culture and craftsmanship. The island, famous for its breathtaking landscapes and millennia-old history, offers a mix of elegant boutiques, traditional shops, and charming markets. Whether you're looking for a special souvenir, an exclusive gift, or a luxury item, Santorini has something for everyone.

No matter how much you want to spend, you'll find options for all budgets, from small souvenirs to luxury gifts. We've added a price range, curiosities about the products, and tips on where to shop safely.

What to Buy

10.1 Local Craftsmanship

Handmade Jewelry

Santorini is renowned for its handmade jewelry, often inspired by the colors and shapes of the island. Gold, silver, and gemstones are crafted to create unique pieces, perfect as keepsakes or gifts.

- **Price:** €30-€300 (or more for exclusive pieces).
- **Curiosity:** Many pieces incorporate stones such as obsidian, found on the island.
- **Where to buy:** Poniros Jewelry in Oia is famous for its modern and traditional designs.

Hand-Painted Ceramics

Handmade items such as hand-painted ceramics and traditional fabrics are perfect for decorating your home or as gifts.

- **Price:** €15-€200, depending on size and complexity of the design.

- **Curiosity:** Many ceramics feature motifs from ancient Cycladic civilizations.
- **Where to buy**: AK Ceramics in Firostefani is a renowned workshop for quality pieces.

Volcanic Lava Items

- **Price:** €20-€150 for sculptures and jewelry.
- **Curiosity:** Each piece is unique, made with materials collected directly from the volcano.
- **Where to buy**: Earth & Water in Pyrgos specializes in volcanic material items.

10.2 Original Souvenirs: Small Gifts, Big Memories

Soaps and Natural Cosmetics
- **Price:** €3-€15 for soaps; €10-€40 for creams and oils.
- **Curiosity:** Essential oils often include lavender, rosemary, or local citrus.
- **Where to buy:** BioAroma in Fira is a reliable source for natural products.

Photographs and Author Prints
- **Price:** €10-€100 for prints; €50-€500 for original artworks.
- **Curiosity:** Some photographers include a certificate of authenticity with their works.
- **Where to buy**: Art of the Loom Gallery in Fira is perfect for collectors.

Leather Sandals
- **Price:** €30-€70, depending on design and craftsmanship
- **Curiosity:** Many designs are inspired by ancient Greek models.
- **Where to buy**: Sandal Workshop in Fira is known for its quality sandals.

10.3 Flavors of Santorini: From Everyday Food to Gourmet   Gifts

Volcanic Wines
- **Price:** €10-€60 per bottle, depending on the winery and label.
- **Curiosity:** The Assyrtiko grape, typical of the island, grows in kouloura, a technique that weaves the vines into low circles to protect them from the wind and sun.
- **Where to buy:**
- Santo Wines (near Pyrgos): offers stunning views of the caldera and tastings.
- Hatzidakis Winery: for those who love organic and authentic products.

Santorini Capers

- **Price:** €5-€10 for a small jar.
- **Curiosity:** Their unique flavor comes from the volcanic soil and the scarcity of water.
- **Where to buy:** In local markets or specialized shops like Canava Santorini.

Dried Tomatoes and Yellow Fava

- **Price:** €4-€8 for dried tomatoes; €3-€7 for yellow fava.
- **Curiosity:** Yellow fava is not a type of broad bean but a legume similar to lentils, grown on the island for thousands of years.
- **Where to buy:** Spicy Bites in Fira has an excellent selection.

Where to Shop in Peace

- *Fira*: The capital is the heart of shopping, with shops for all budgets. Visit the central market for affordable local products.

- *Oia*: Known for its chic style, Oia is ideal for those looking for exclusive items. Here you'll find art galleries, fashion shops, and high-end jewelry for an elegant shopping experience.

- *Emporio and Pyrgos*: For a more authentic atmosphere, traditional villages offer genuine products away from the crowds. Here, you'll find local markets and traditional shops with affordable prices.

10.4 Tips for Shopping Without Surprises

1. *Beware of Imitations*: Especially for jewelry and craftsmanship, trust reputable shops.

2. *Watch Out for Customs*: If you purchase food products or wine, check the rules for importing them into your country.

Customs Tips: What You Need to Know
When returning from Santorini to Italy, it's helpful to know a few rules to avoid unpleasant surprises at customs. Even though Greece is part of the European Union, there are some limitations on certain products. Here are the details for Italian travelers:

Food Products

1. *Wine and Alcoholic Beverages*
   Limits: You can carry up to 90 liters of wine (of which a maximum of 60 liters can be sparkling wine) and 10 liters of spirits. For beer, the limit is 110 liters.
   Tip: Despite the high limits, only bring what you can comfortably carry, avoiding fragile packaging.

2. *Typical Products (Capers, Dried Tomatoes, Yellow Fava)*
   Always ask for the receipt: It's not only for a possible refund but also as a guarantee of the product's authenticity.
   Rules: You can bring packaged or vacuum-sealed food for personal use without any specific restrictions.
   Tip: Keep food sealed in your suitcase to avoid liquid or odor leaks.

Objects and Craftsmanship

1. *Ceramics and Local Craftsmanship*
   Rules: There are no restrictions on handcrafted items, but make sure they are not archaeological artifacts or imitations of them, as these are subject to strict regulations.
   Tip: Always keep the receipt to prove the purchase is legitimate.

2. *Jewelry*
   Rules: If you carry valuable jewelry, it's advisable to declare it at customs to avoid issues in case of inspection.
   Tip: Bring a document certifying the value or provenance of the jewelry (invoice or certificate of authenticity).

Liquids and Cosmetics

Rules for Hand Luggage

* Liquids, including wine and cosmetics, must be carried in bottles of a maximum of 100 ml each, placed in a transparent, resealable bag (1 liter total capacity).

* Tip: For larger items (wine, oil, etc.), use checked luggage.

How Much Can You Spend?

There are no specific limits for the value of goods purchased between EU countries, as long as they are for personal use and not for resale.

However:

Suspicious Quantities: If you transport a large number of the same product (e.g., 20 bottles of wine), you may be asked to prove they are for personal use.

Other Useful Tips

1. *Transporting Fragile Bottles*:

   - Use a padded wine bag or wrap the bottles in clothes to protect them.
   - Many wineries in Santorini offer secure packaging for air travel.

2. *What to Avoid*:

   - Don't buy historical artifacts or items that seem antique without legal certification: they may be confiscated.
   - Don't transport seeds or plants without authorization: some species may be prohibited.

3. *Baggage Insurance*:

   - If transporting valuable items (jewelry, artworks), consider baggage insurance.

11. Useful Numbers and Emergency Contacts

To make the most of your experience in Santorini, it's important to be prepared for any eventuality. Below you'll find a list of useful numbers and contacts for medical emergencies, pharmacies, and other essential services. Save this page to your favorites so you always have it on hand!

General Emergencies

- **European emergency number:** 112
- **Police:** 100
- **Ambulance:** 166
- **Fire department:** 199
- **Tourist Police:** 171

Medical Assistance

- **Fira Health Center** (24/7): +30 22860 35300
- **Fira Private Clinic:** +30 22860 21728

Main Pharmacies

- **Fira:** +30 22860 22700
- **Kamari:** +30 22860 32440
- **Messaria:** +30 22860 32566

Transport and Local Support

- **Taxi (Fira):** +30 22860 22555
- **Public buses (Fira):** +30 22860 25404/25462
- **Port authority:** +30 22860 22239

Tips for Minor Accidents

For cuts, abrasions, or jellyfish stings, go directly to one of the indicated pharmacies or contact the health center in Fira. The island's pharmacies are well-stocked and can often offer immediate assistance or guidance on the next steps.

Further Information

Feel free to contact the Tourist Police at number 171 for any doubts or support needs.

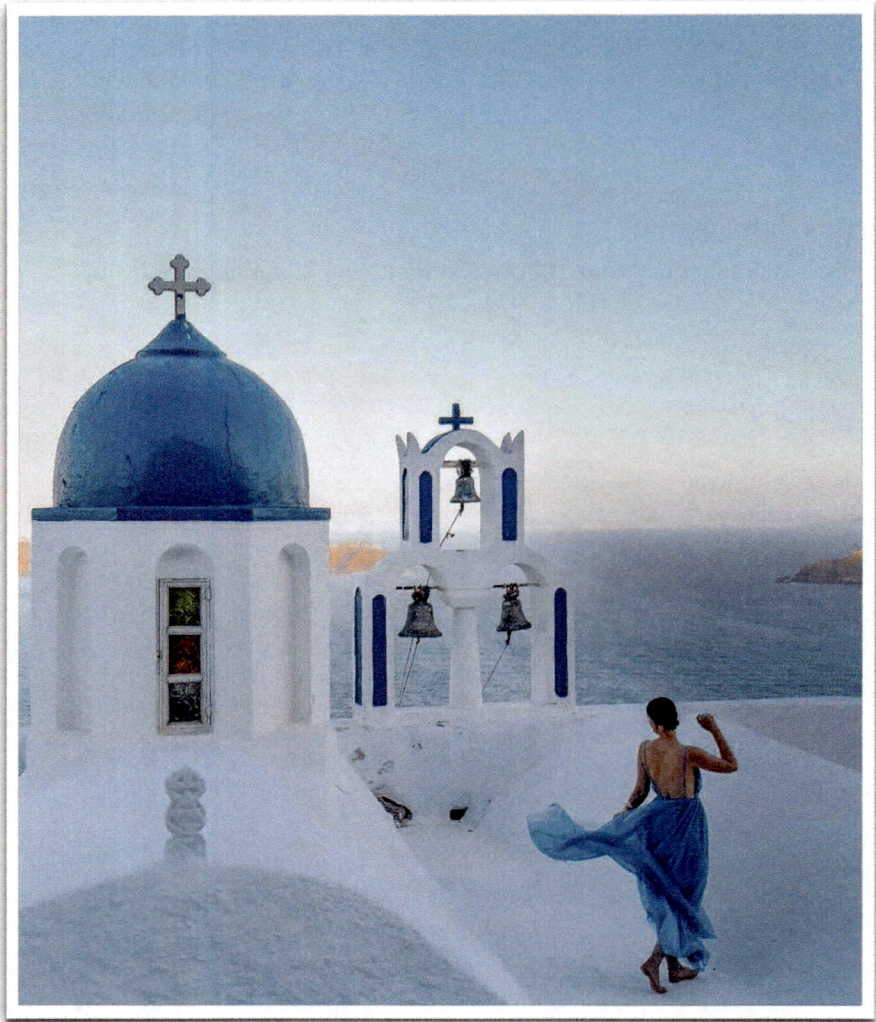

Conclusion: Santorini, a Dream Waiting for You

Imagine being there, on a white terrace, with the sun slowly dipping into the endless blue of the Aegean. The air is filled with saltiness and the scent of bougainvillea, and every corner of the island tells an ancient story, seemingly written to enchant you.

Santorini is not just a destination: it's an invitation to dream, to lose yourself in picturesque alleys, to rediscover the pleasure of the little things. It's the taste of volcanic wine that caresses your palate, the warmth of a sunset that embraces you like a promise of happiness.

Prepare to be amazed, to live days in which every moment becomes magic. Santorini is waiting for you, ready to give you emotions that you'll carry with you forever.

Let your journey begin now: open your heart and let this island surprise you.

Printed in Dunstable, United Kingdom